GENEVIEVE'S MANDALAS

Original art by Geneviève Crabe

Published by Amaryllis Creations
www.amarylliscreations.com

ISBN-13: 978-1518691997
ISBN-10: 1518691994

Introduction

Welcome to my first coloring book. I love drawing mandalas. Their symmetry appeal to both my inner artist and my inner math geek.

About Colored Pencils

Colored pencils are a very versatile medium. Good quality pencils are highly pigmented and blendable. I use primarily Prismacolor pencils, which are wax based.

Have a light touch when you color; then you can apply several layers of color, and create smooth blending and shading.

Although I have complete sets of pencils, I find that I always return to a small set of colors.

This is what I have in my portable set:

- Spanish Orange, Orange
- Permanent Red, Crimson Lake, Tuscan Red
- Light Aqua, Aquamarine, Cobalt Turquoise
- Light Cerulean Blue, Cerulean Blue, Indigo Blue
- Rose, Mulberry
- Lilac, Violet
- Limepeel, Olive Green, Dark Green
- Burnt Ochre. Chocolate, Dark Brown
- Back. White
- Cool Grey 20, 50, 70%
- Warm Grey 10, 20, 30, 50%
- French Grey 20, 50, 70%

Please note...

If you are going to color in the book, I recommend putting a sheet of card stock behind the page you are working on.

About Me

Following a thirty-year career in high-tech, I am now devoting my time to artistic pursuits. I am a digital artist, Certified Zentangle® Teacher, a teacher of bead embroidery. My book *How to Make 100 Embroidery Motifs* was published in January 2014, and my first coloring book, *Genevieve's Mandalas*, was published in October 2015.

If you have any questions, you can email me at gcrabe@mac.com.

My Other Products

- More coloring books.

- Geneviève's Mandala Stencils:
  a mandala design kit consists of several circular grid templates.

- Tangle organizers for Zentangle® artists.

- Digital art tutorials on YouTube.

- Brushes for the Procreate digital art app for iPad.

For the latest information, visit my website:

www.amarylliscreations.com

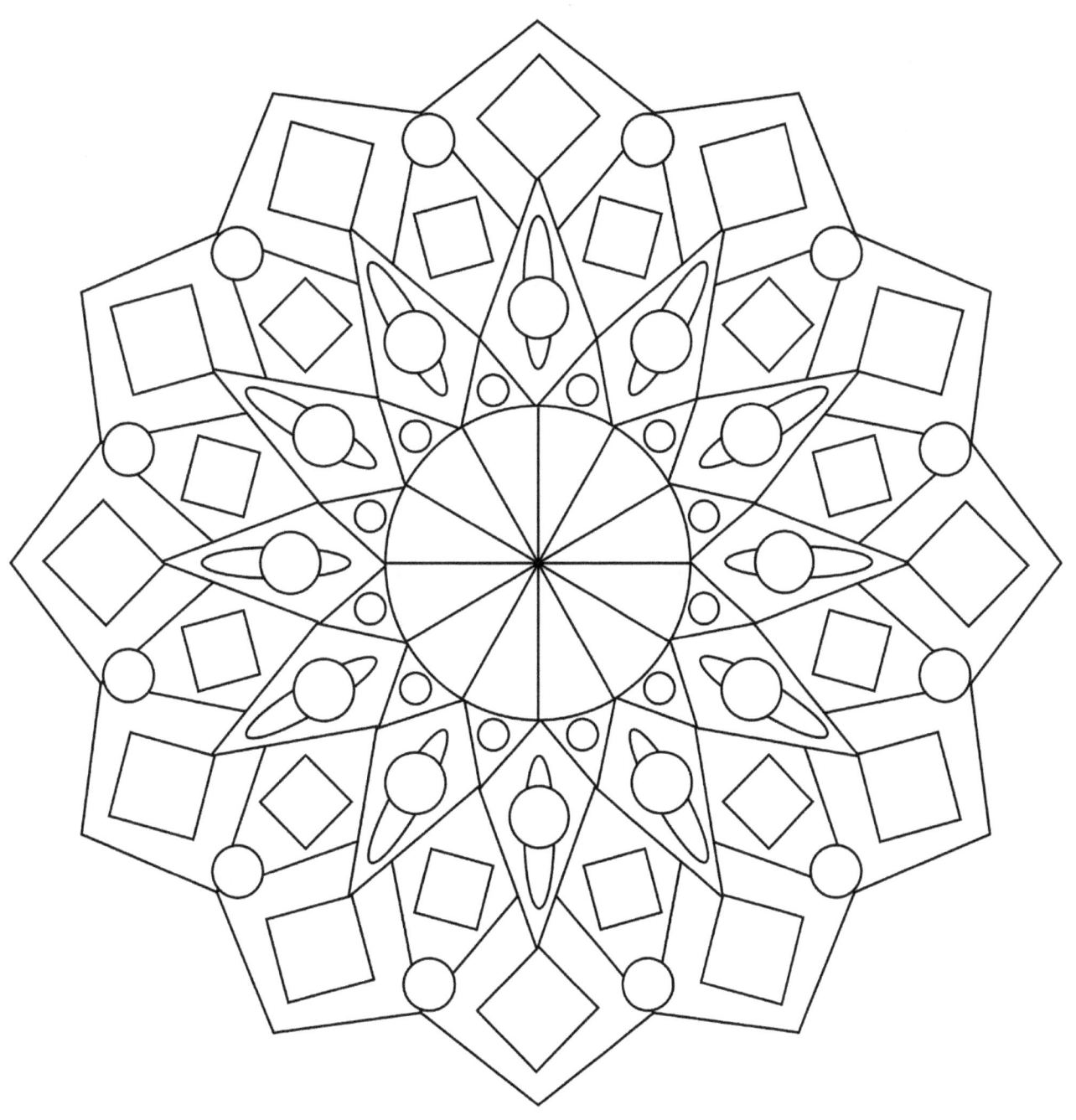

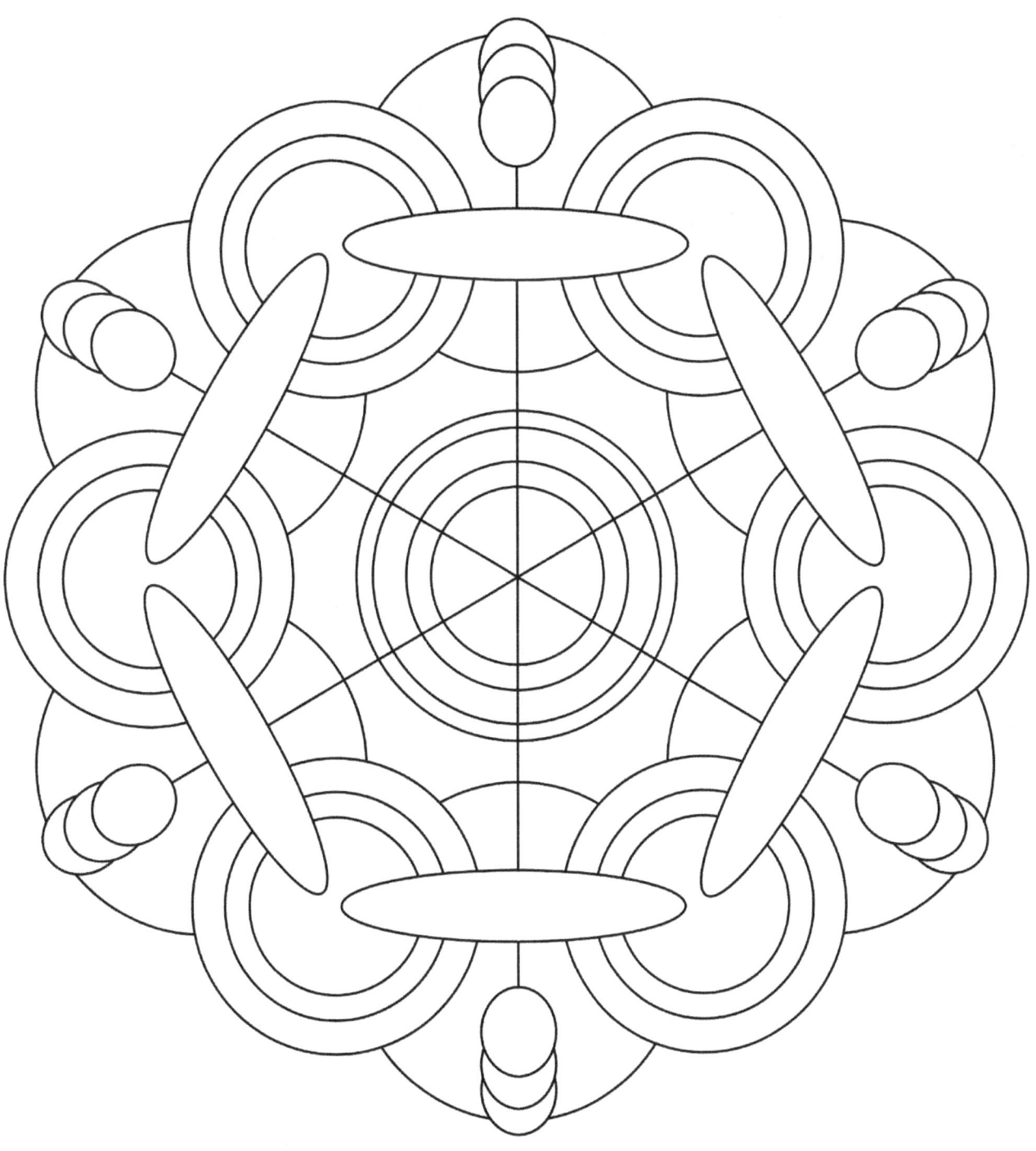

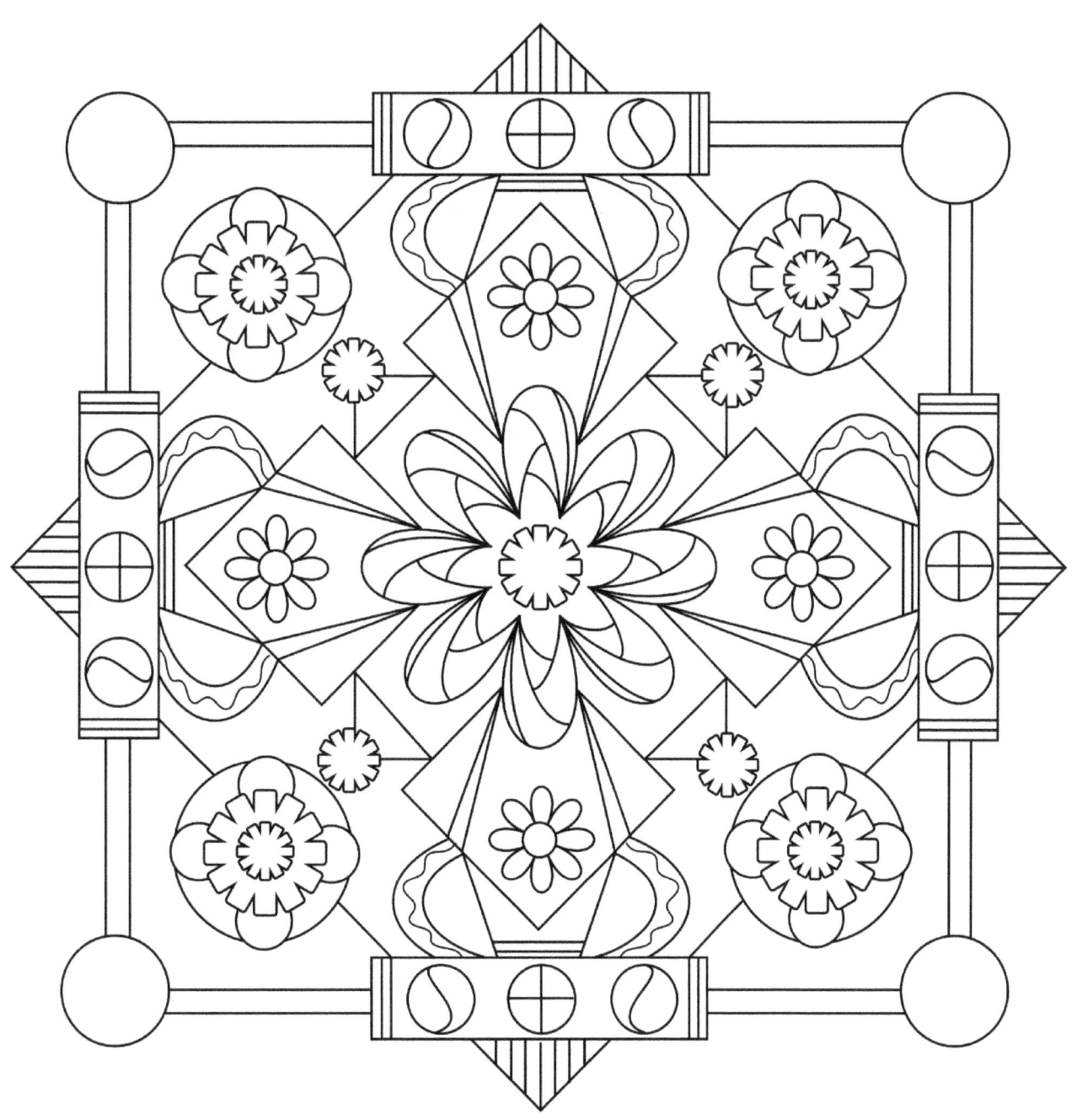

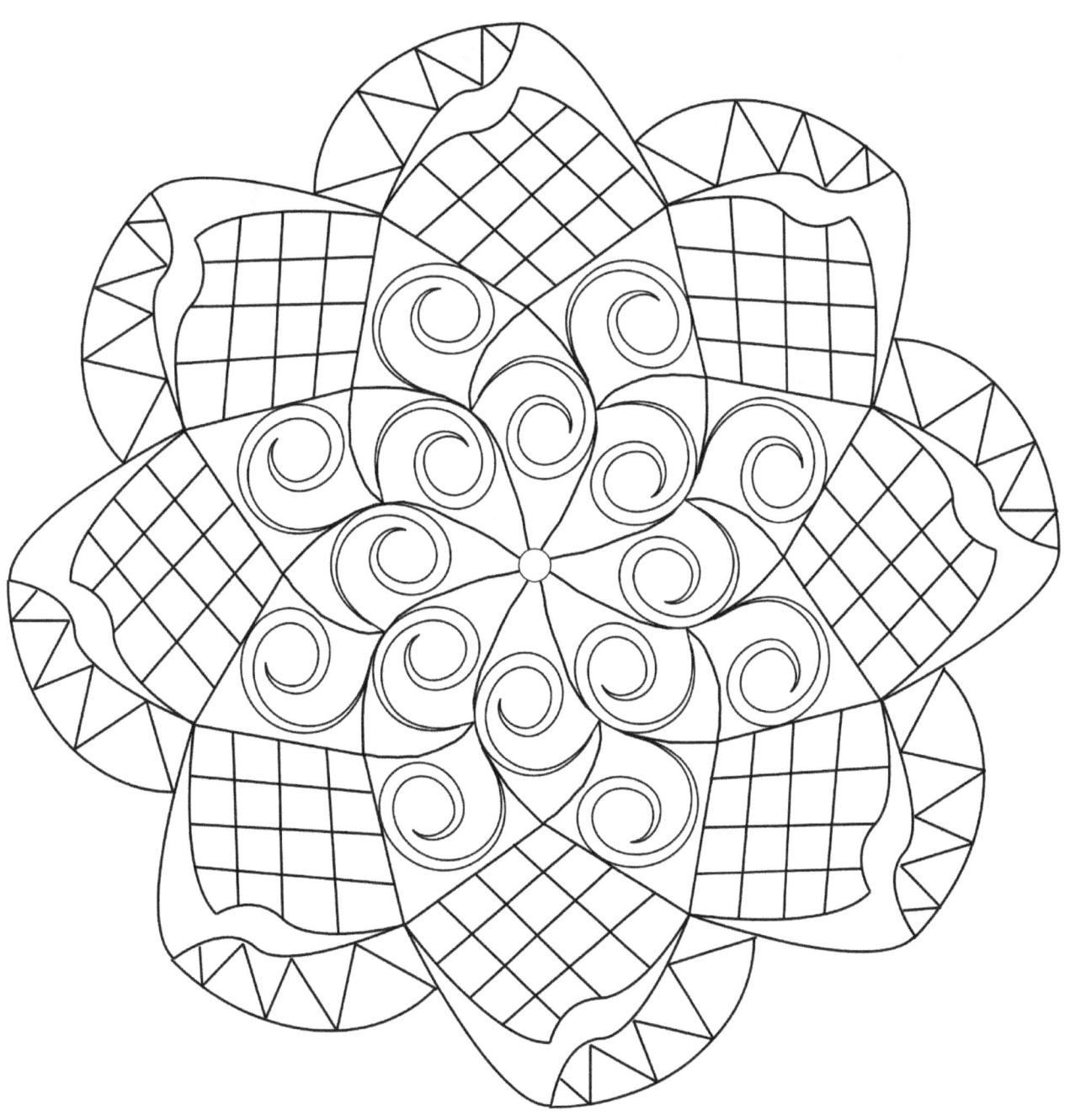

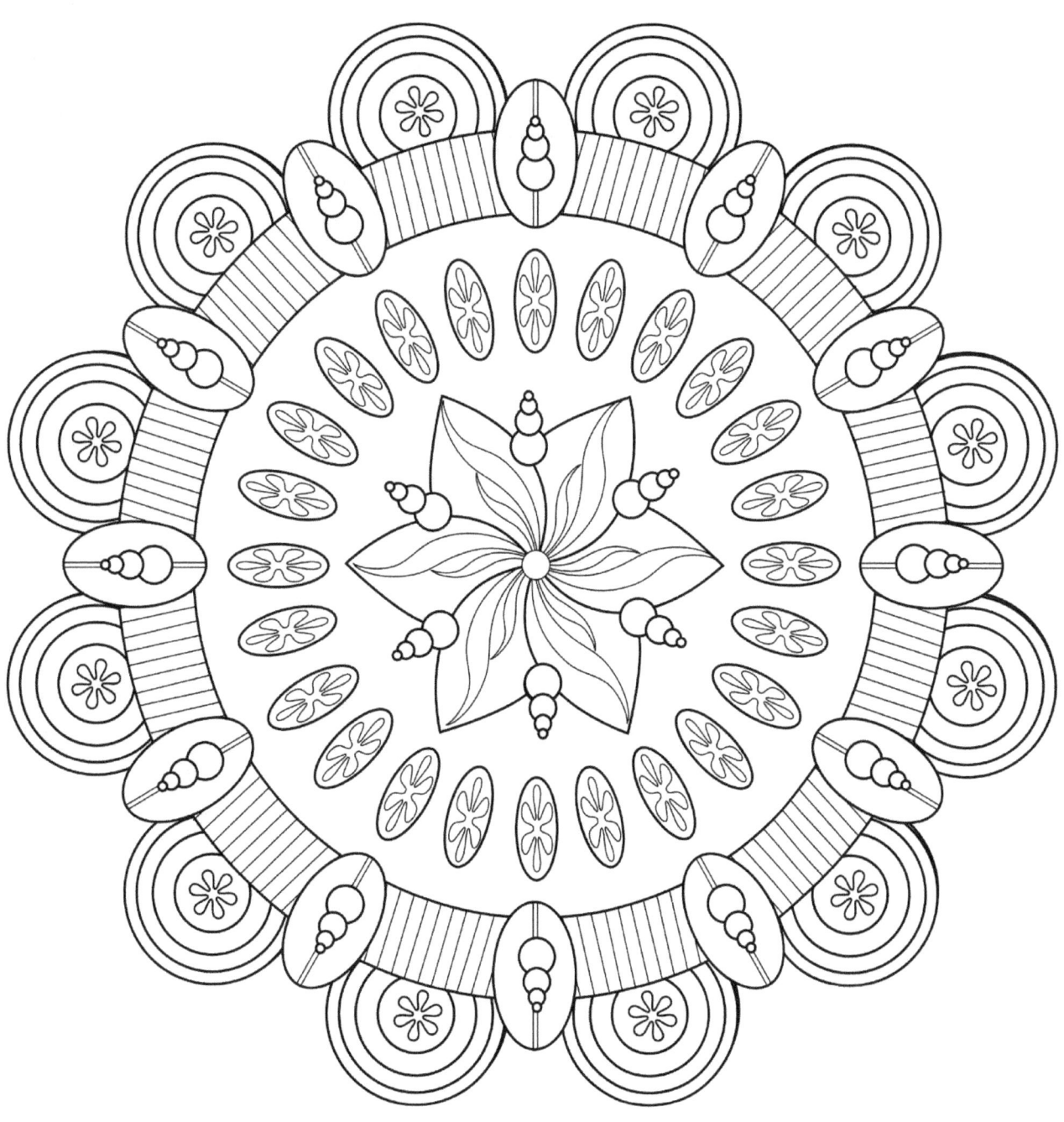

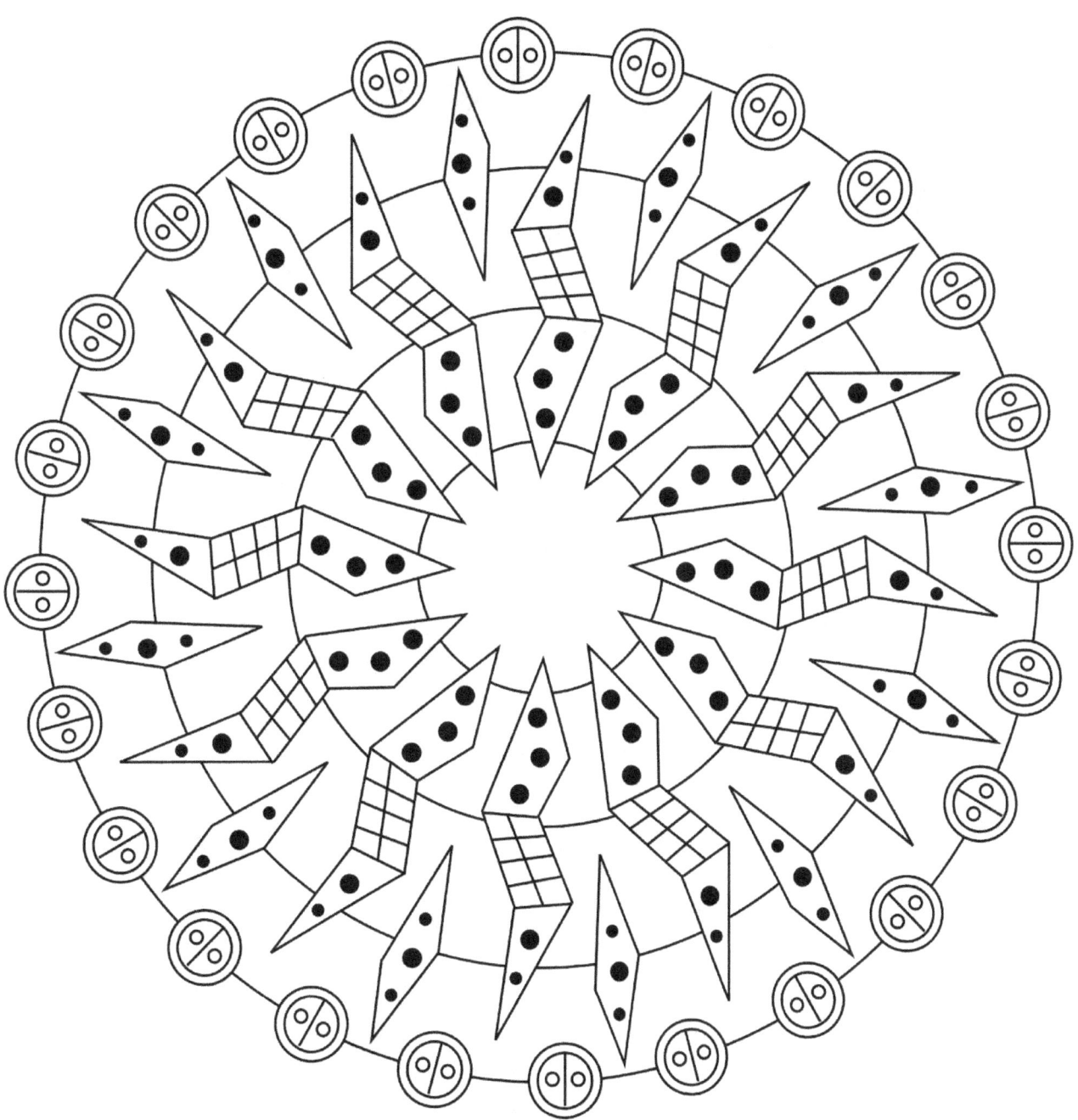

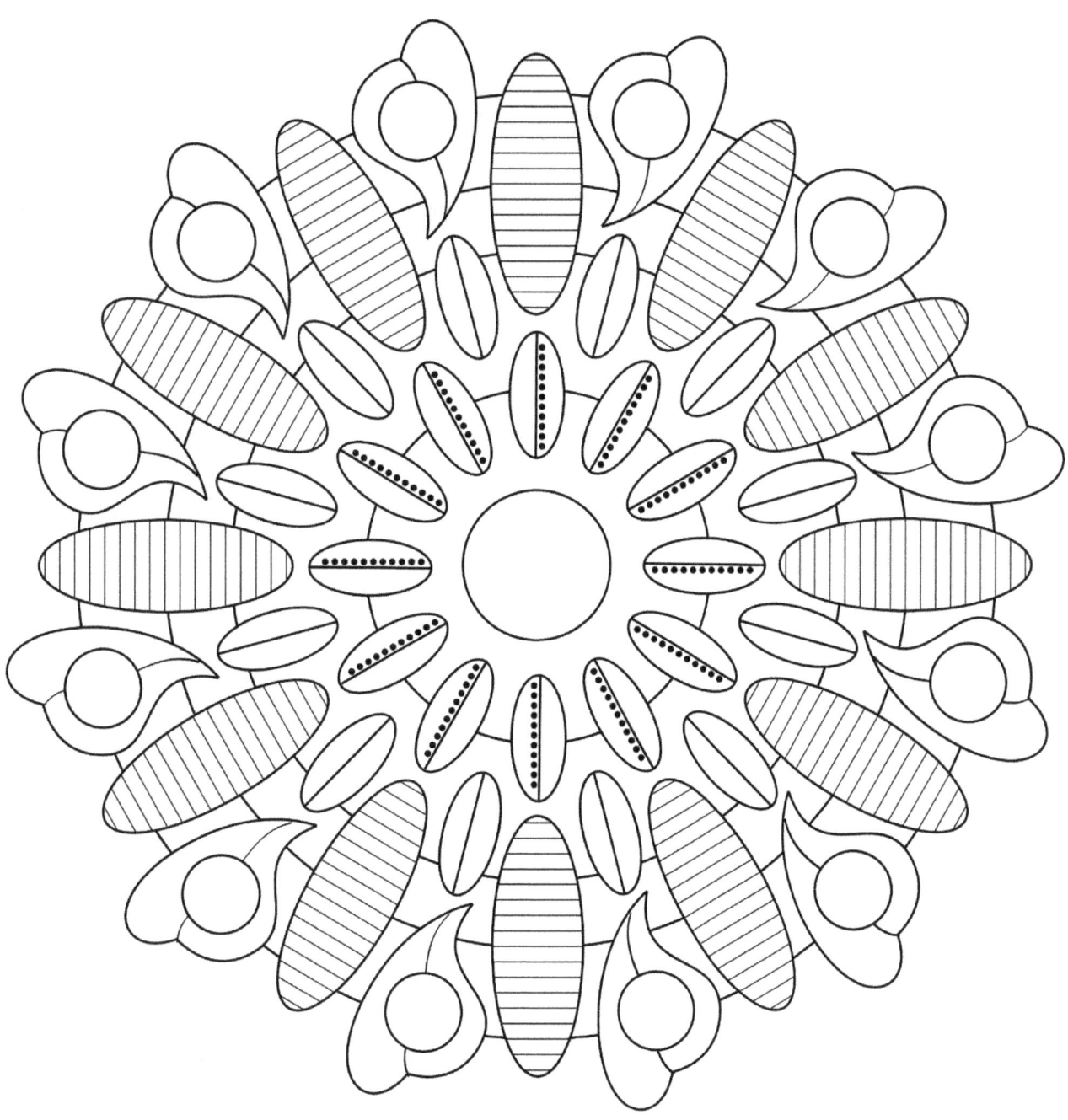

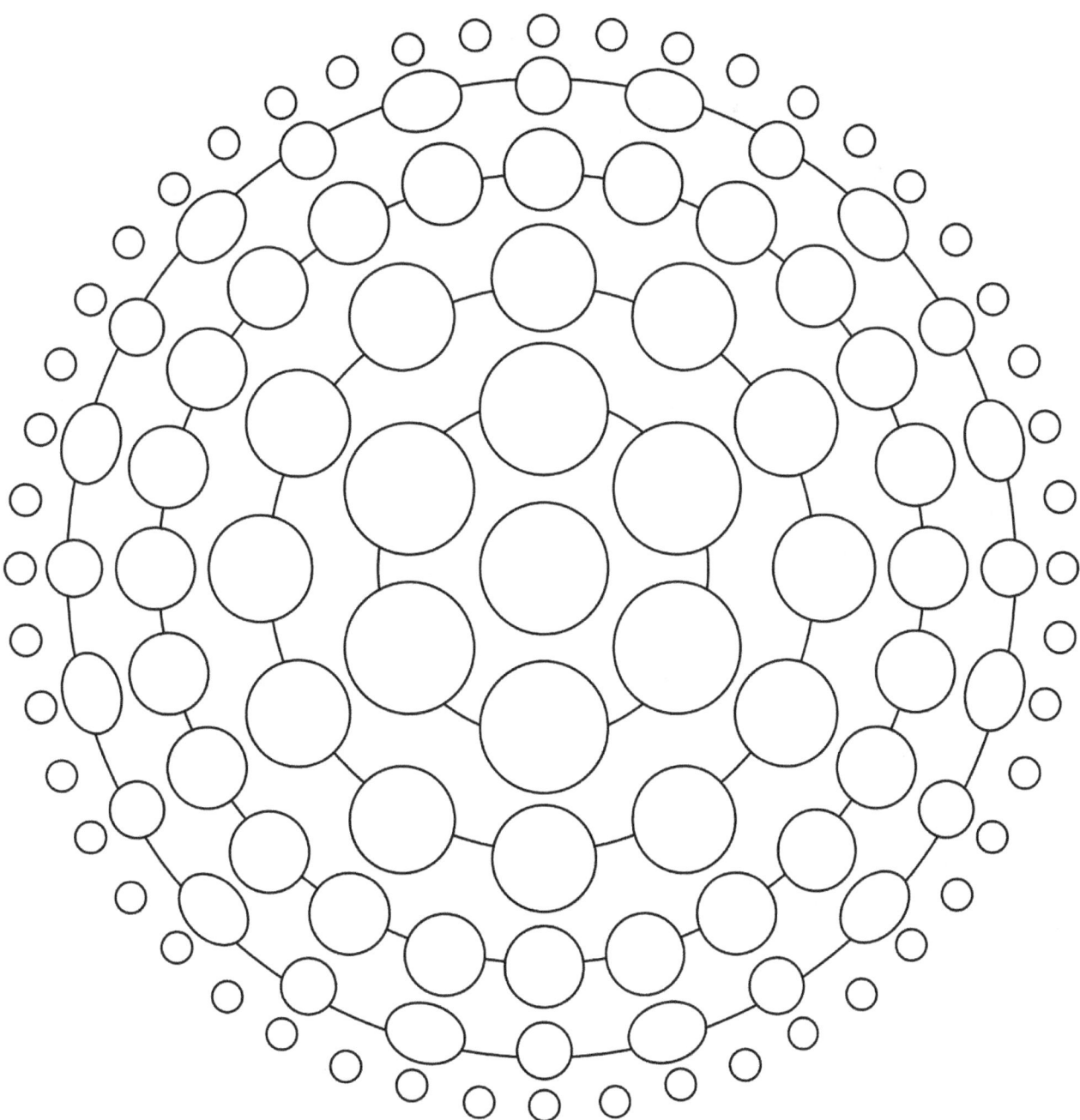

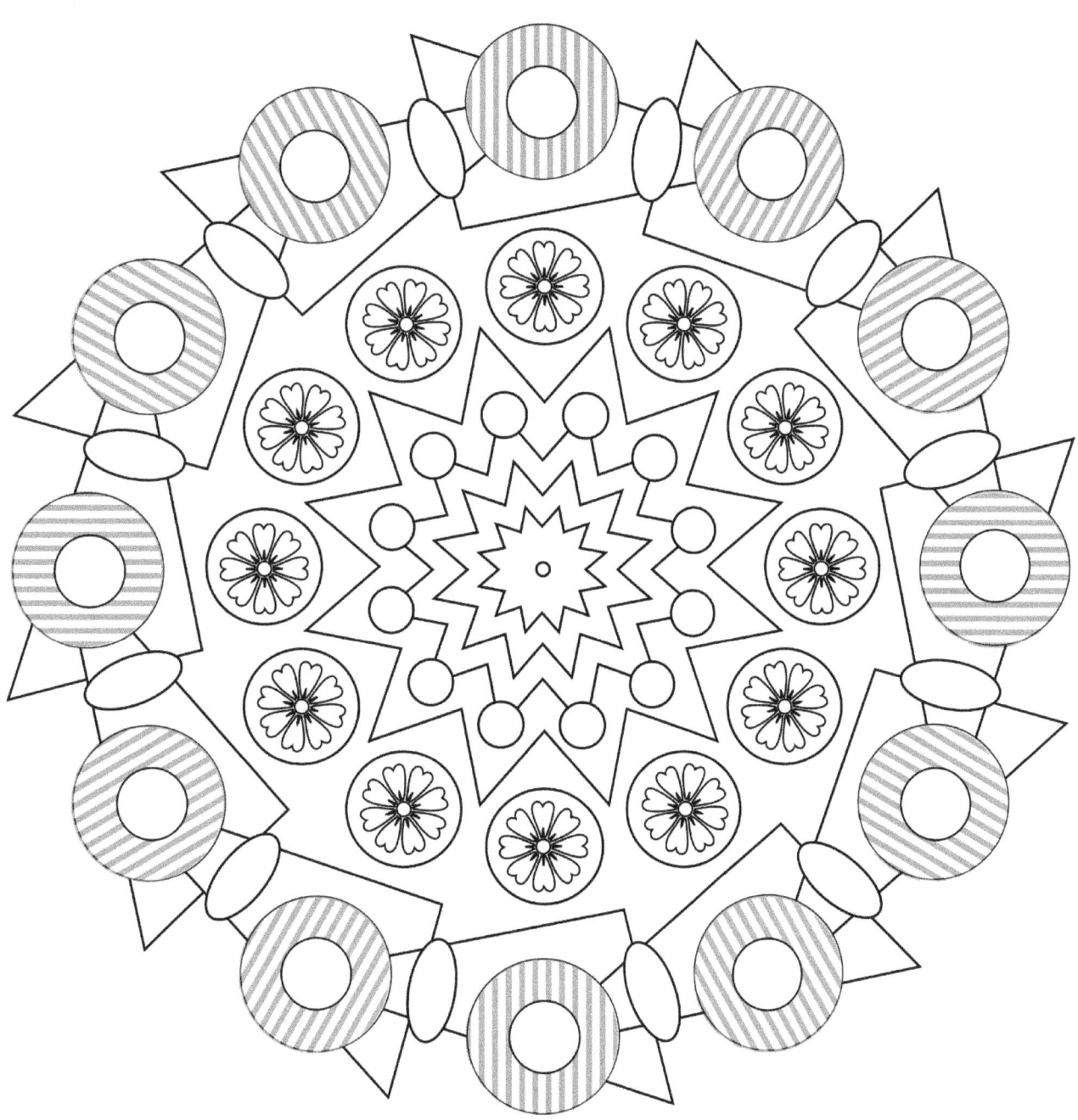

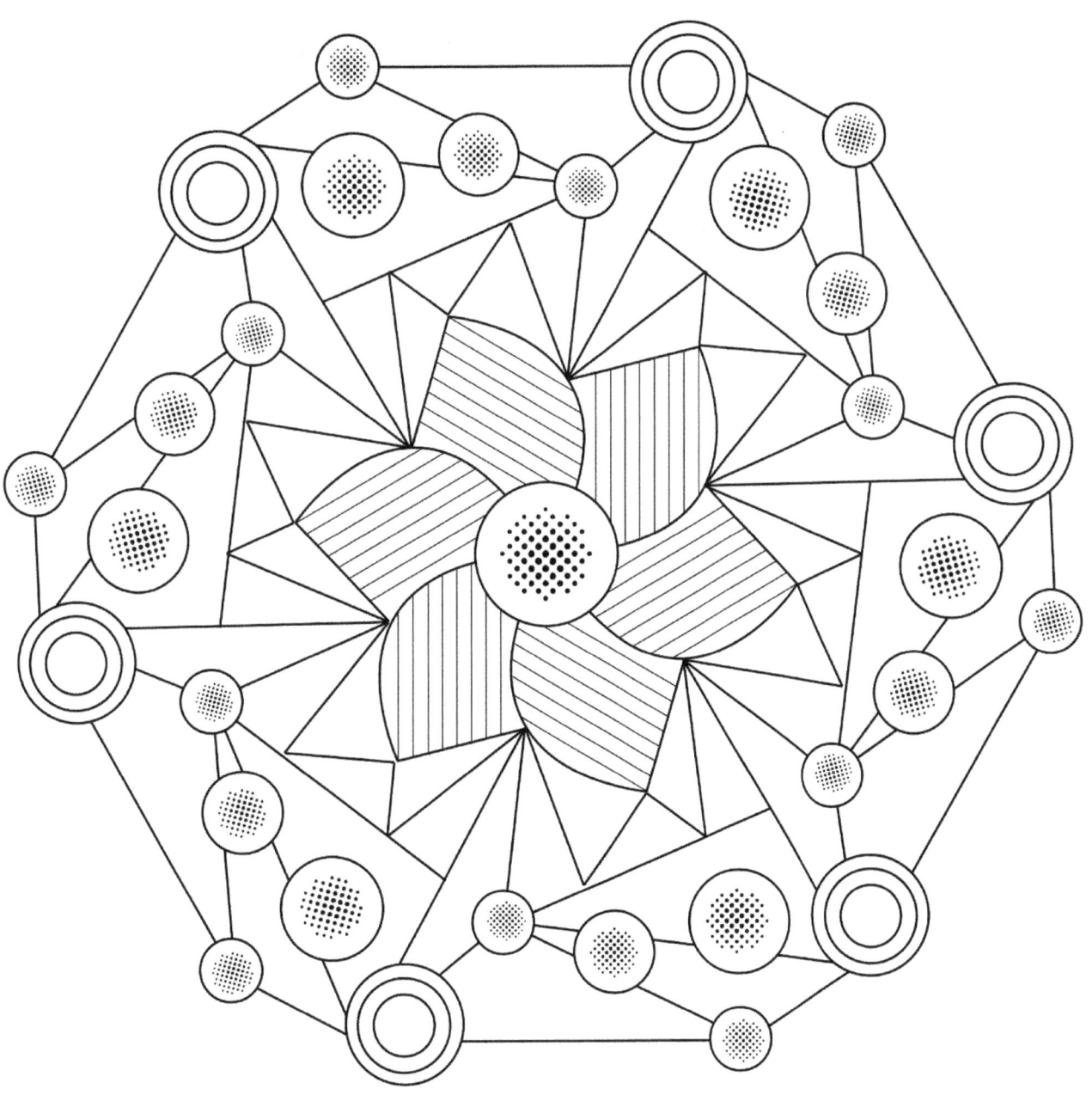

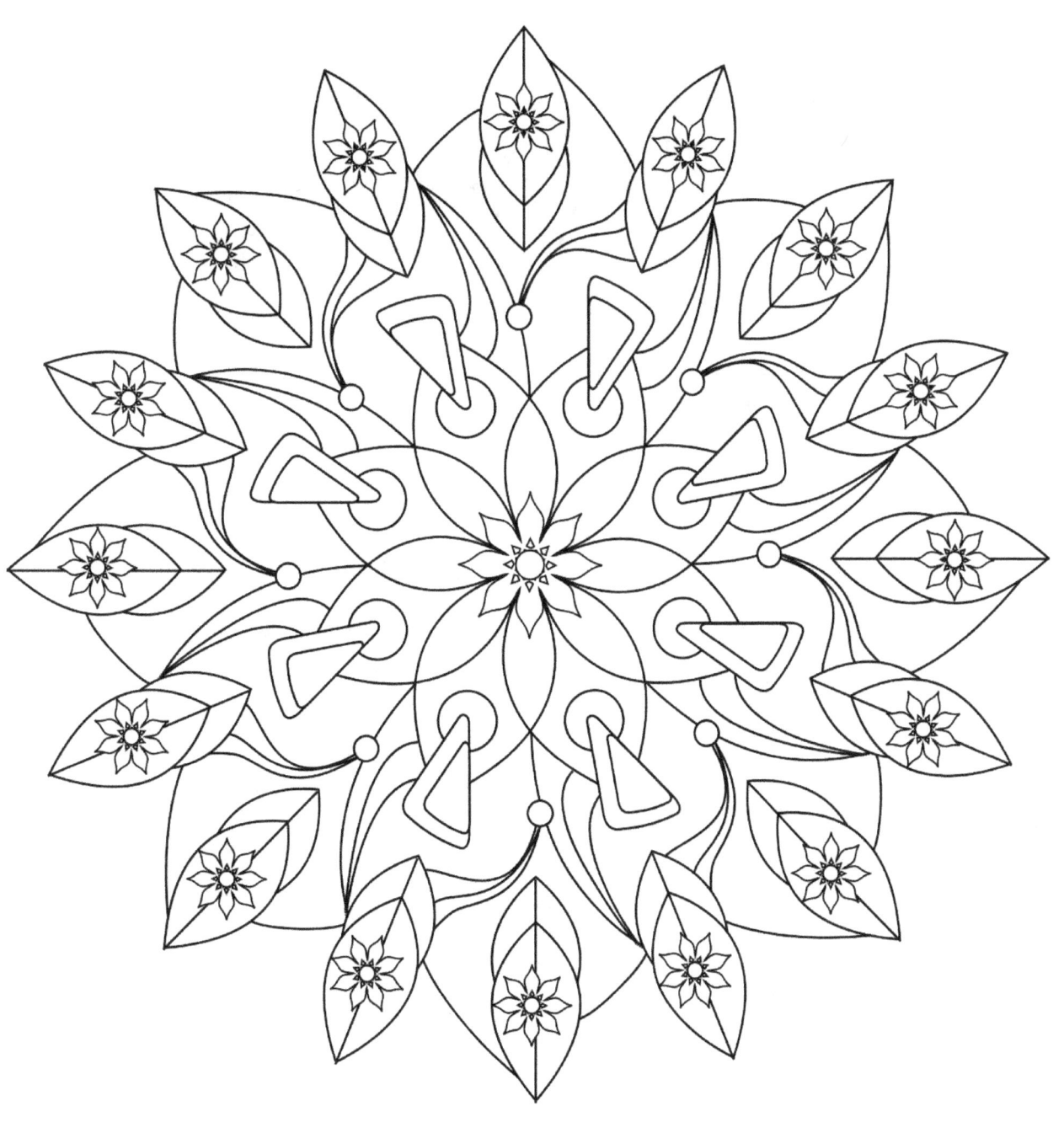

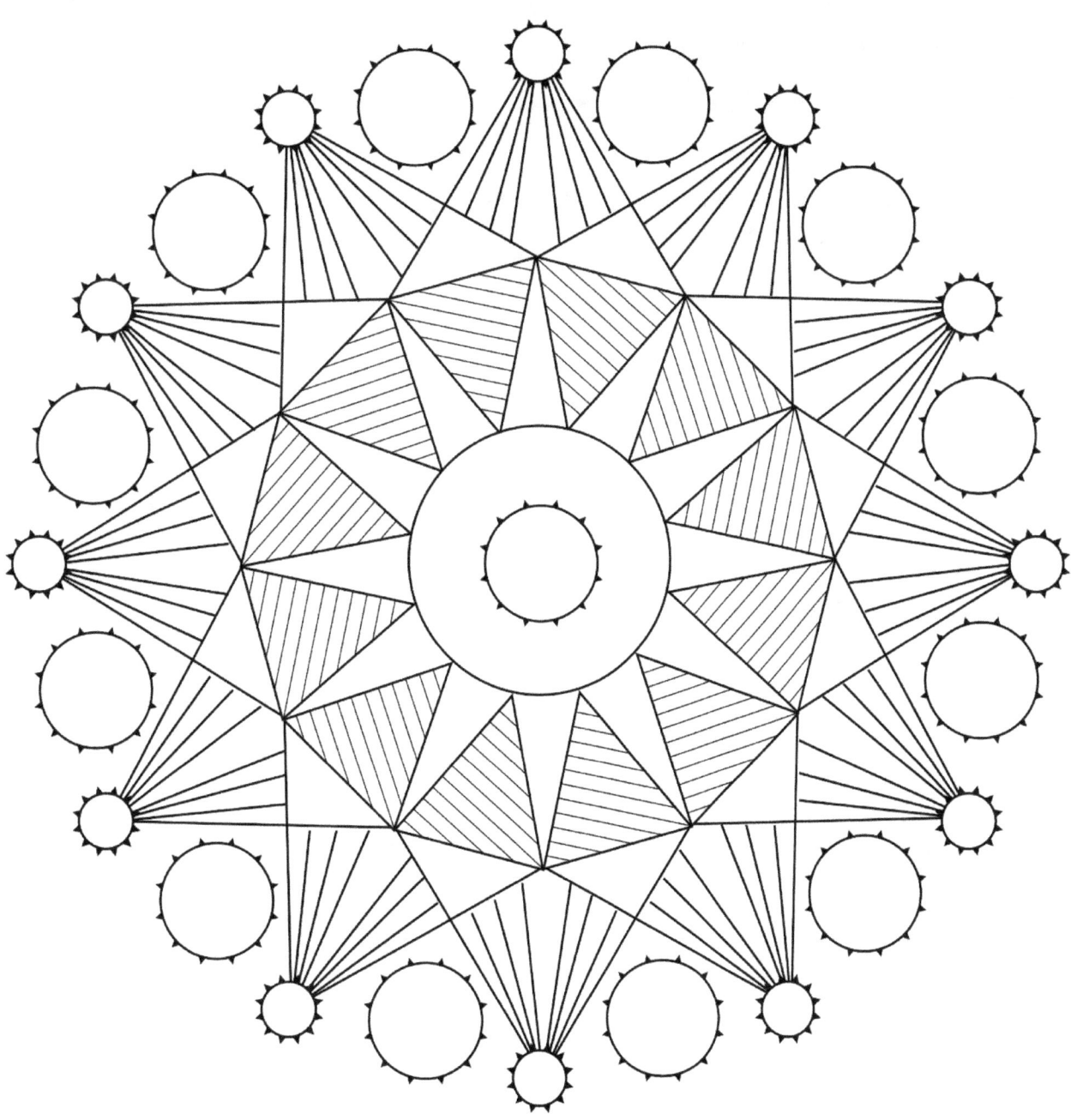

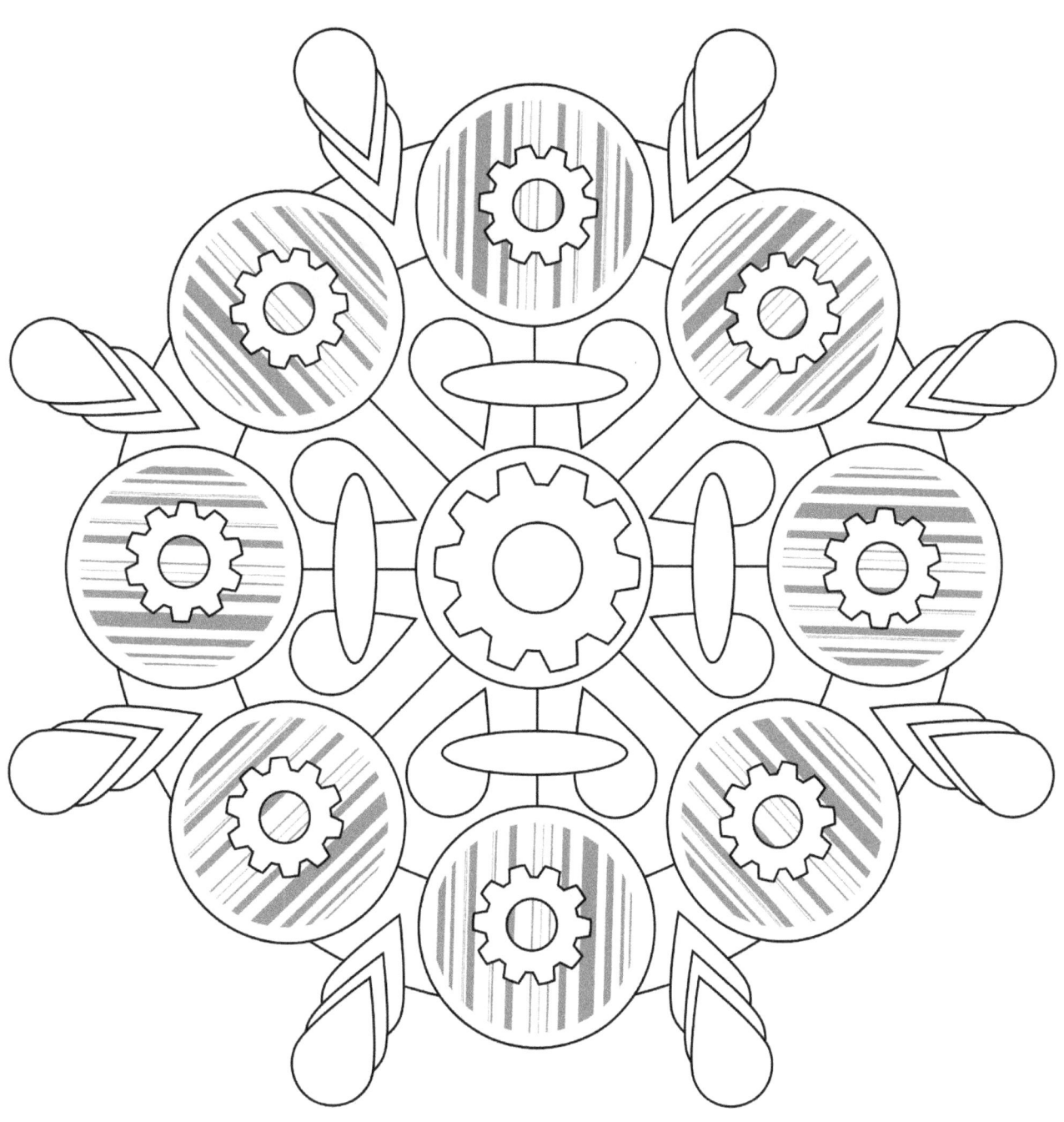

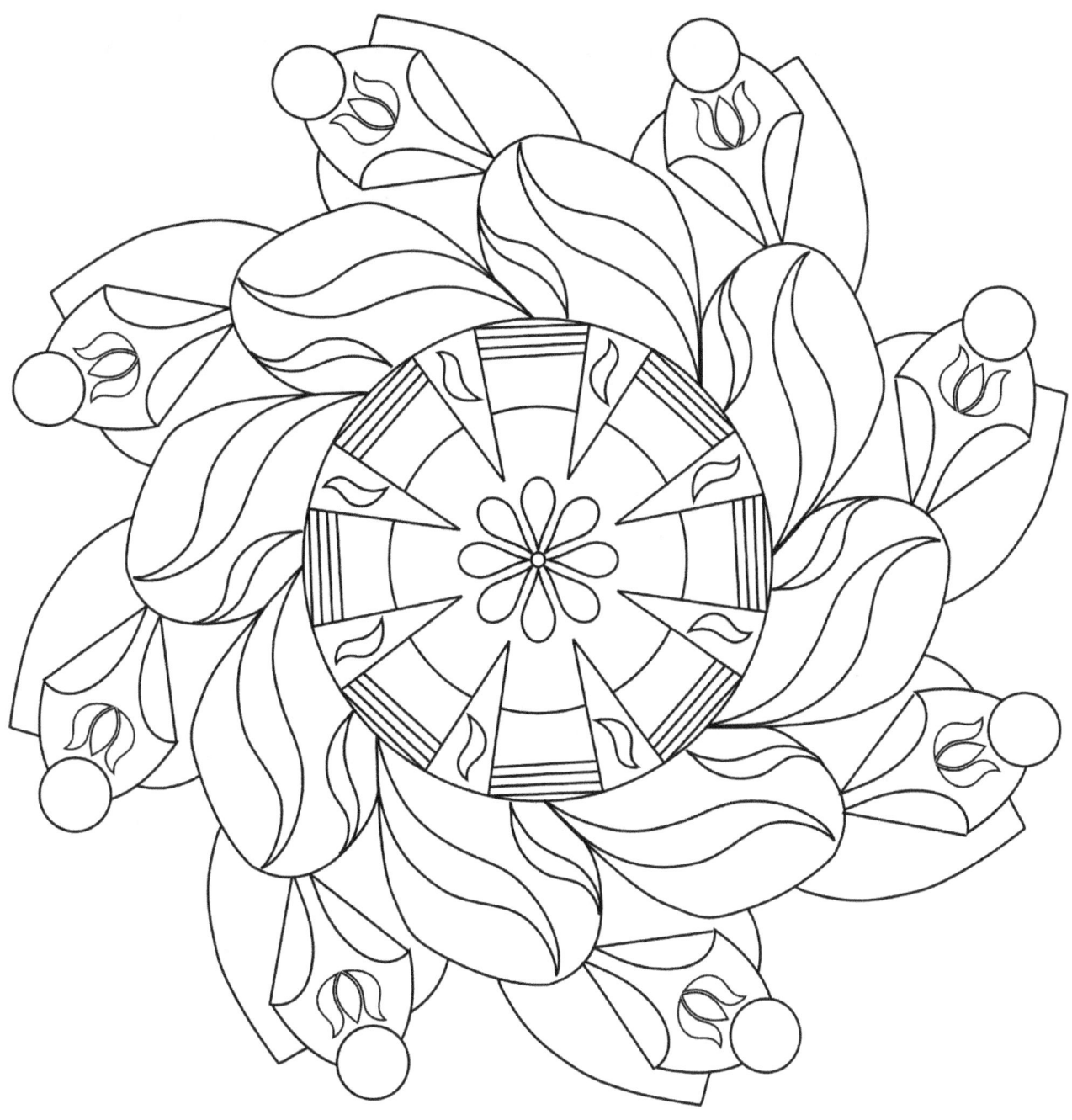

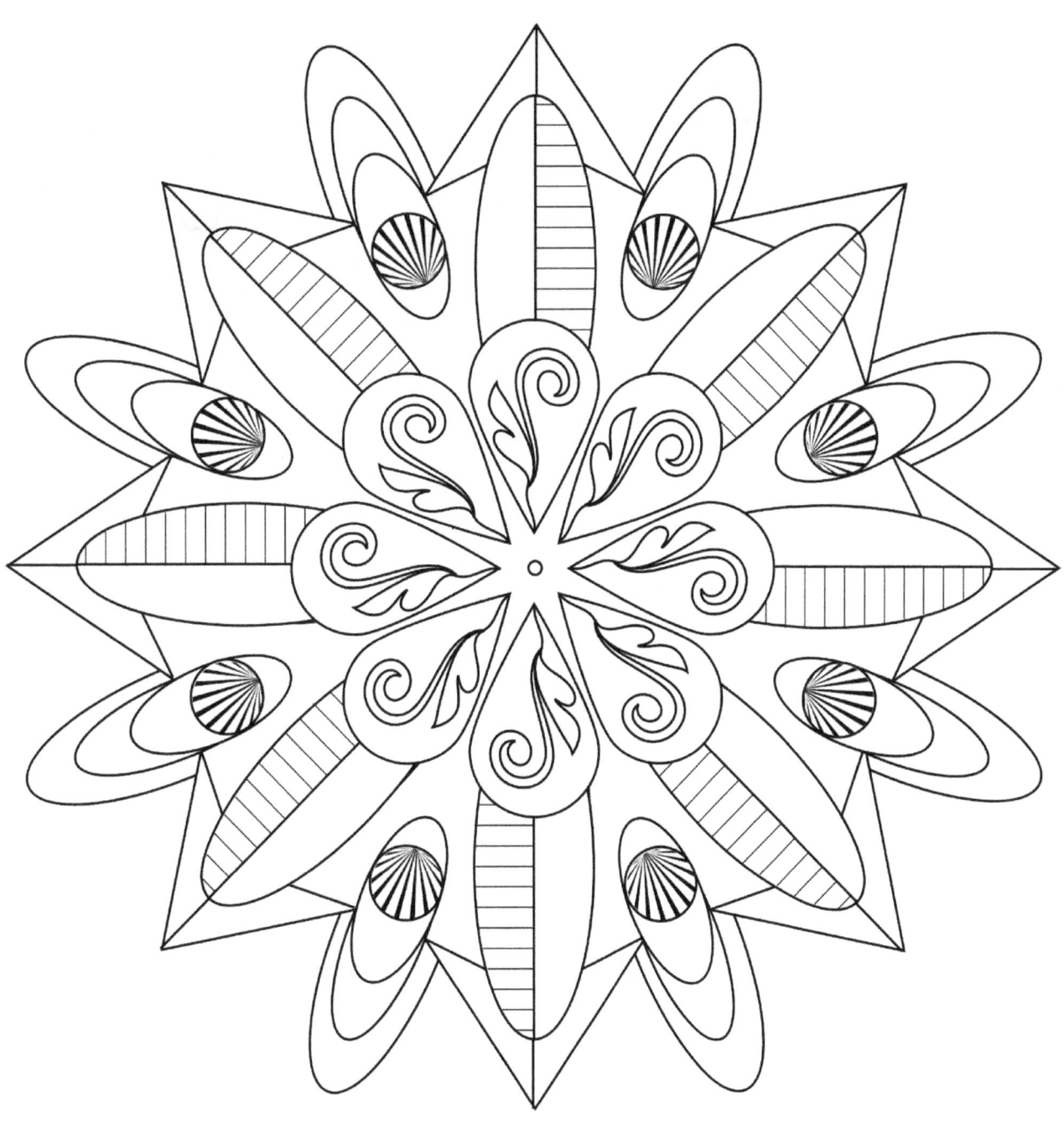

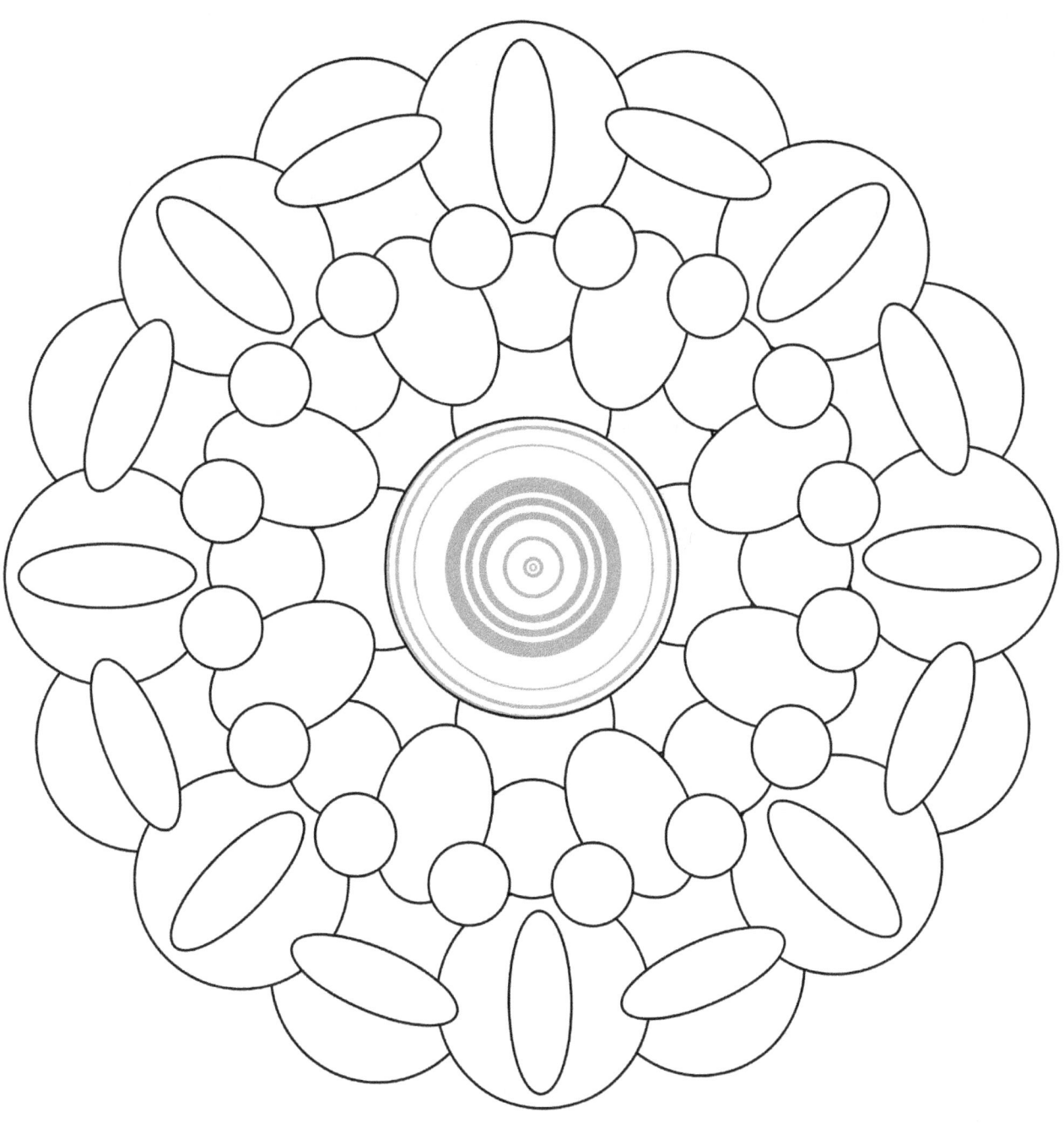

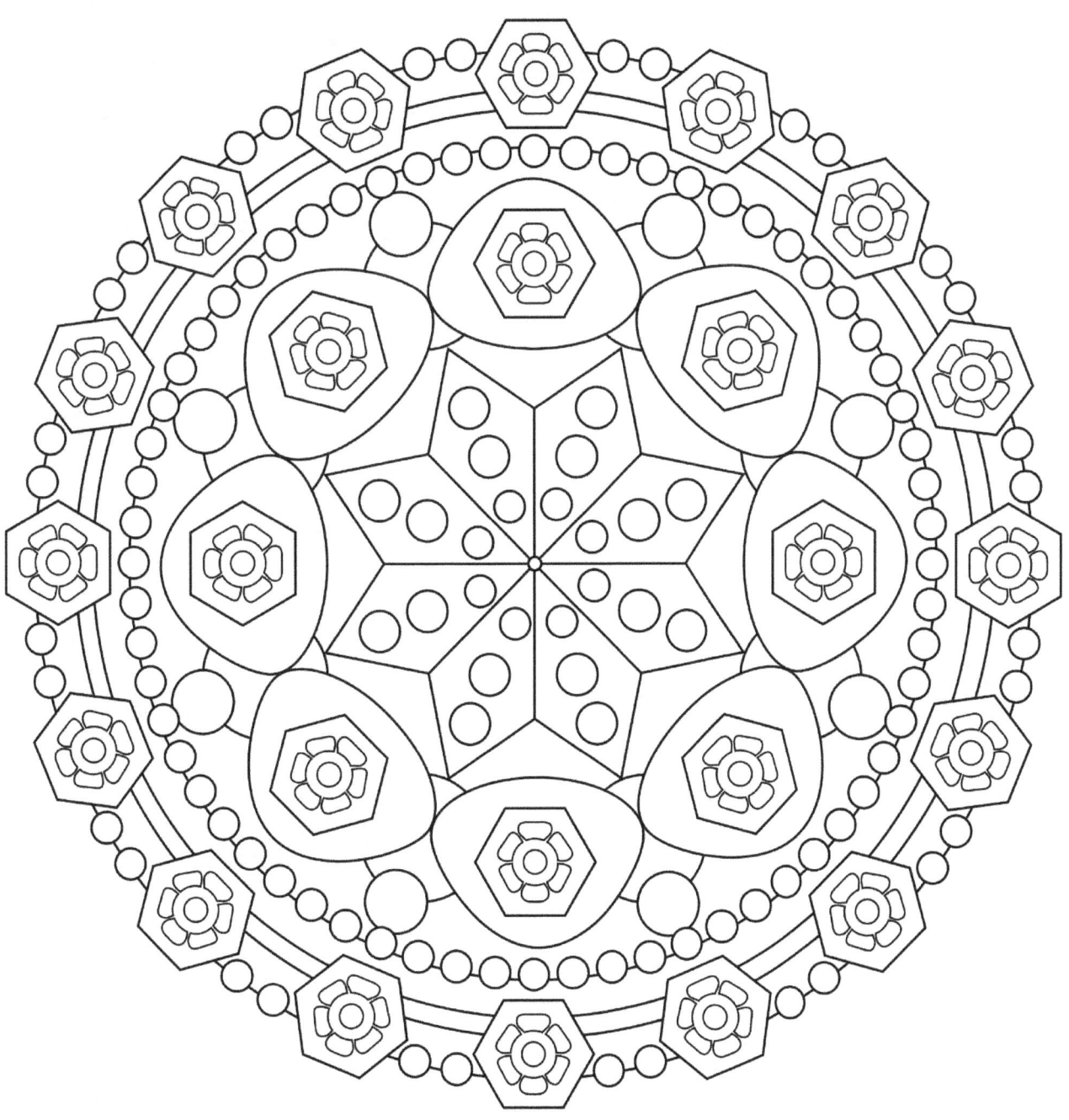

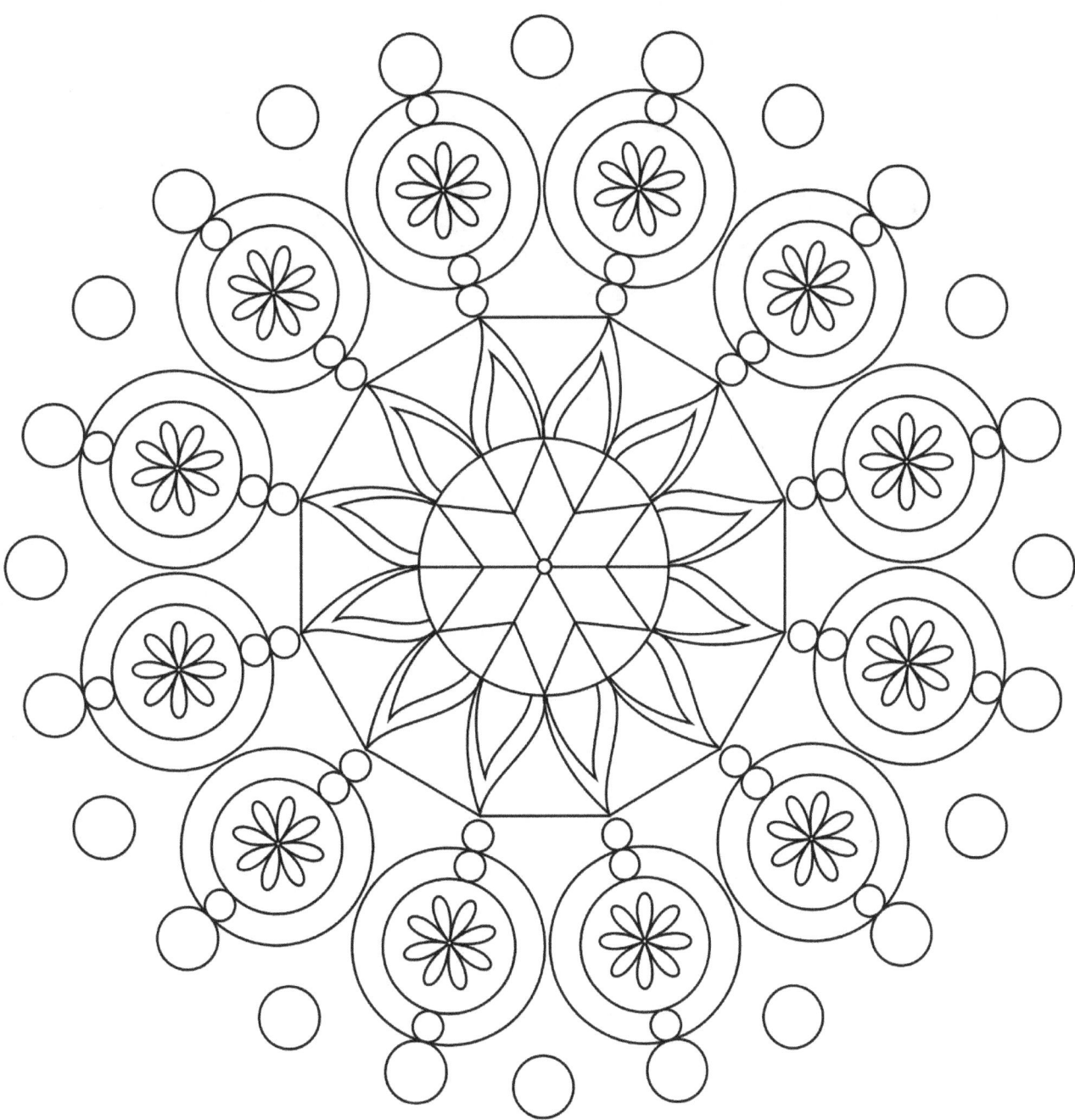

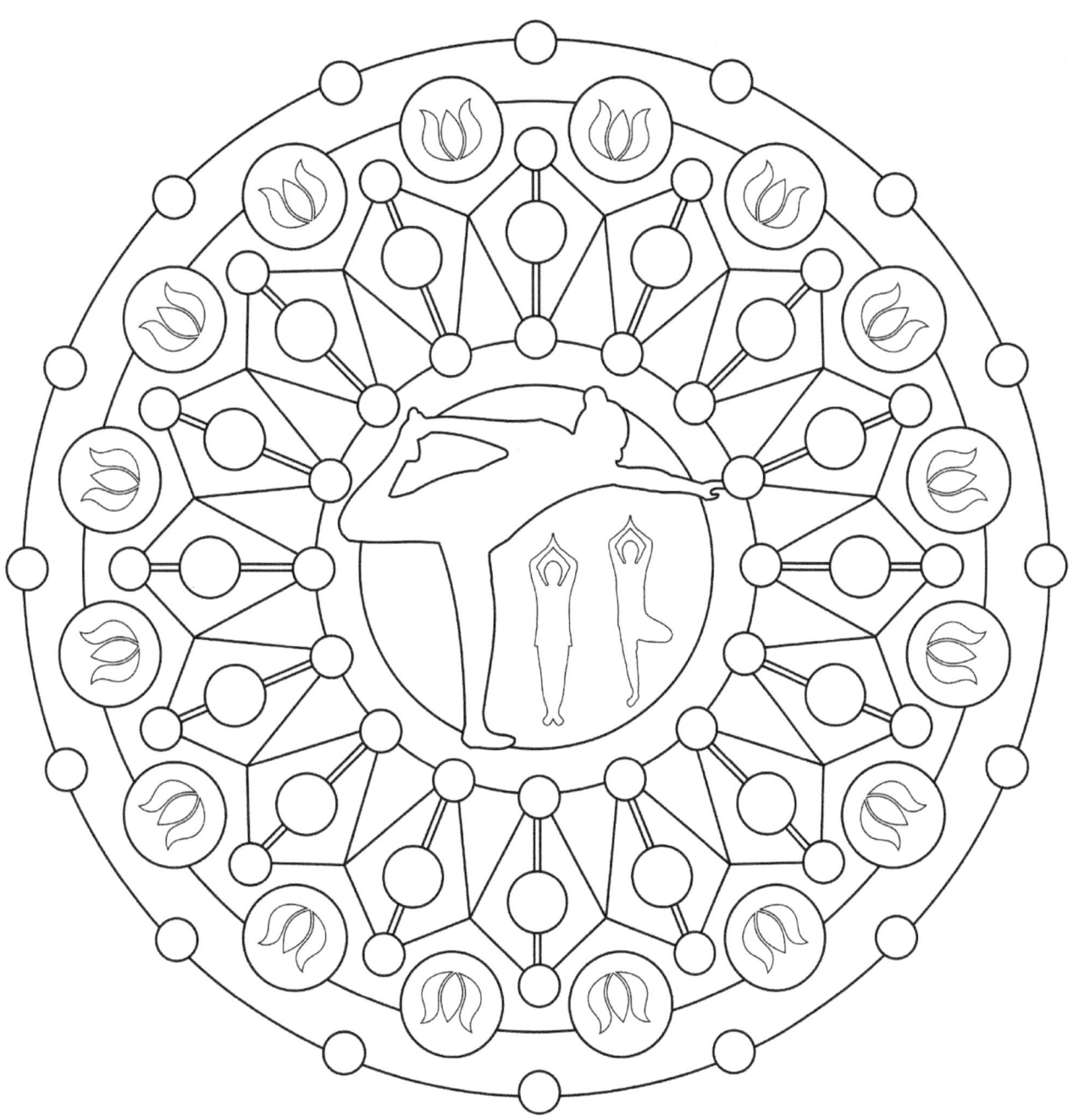

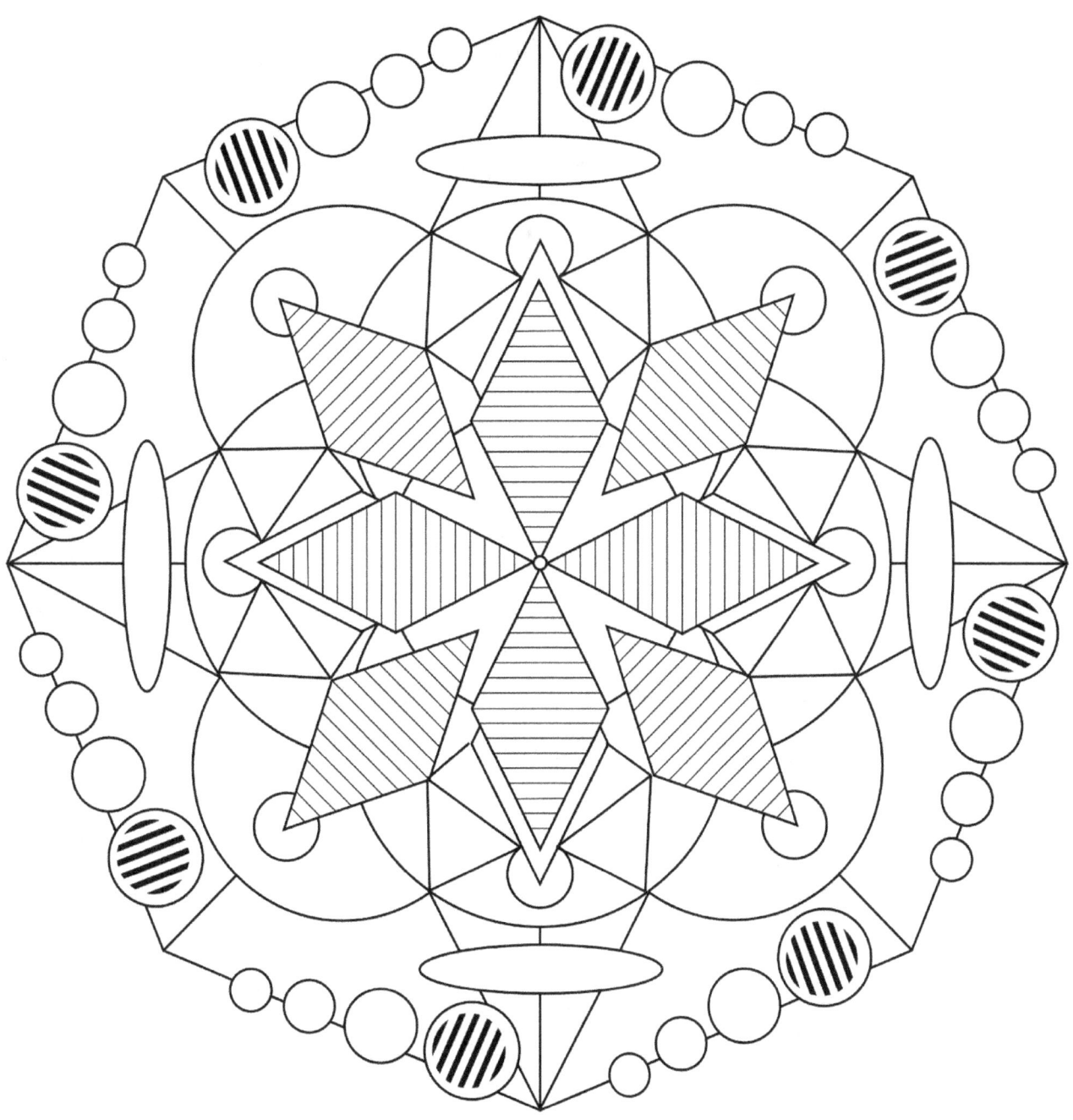

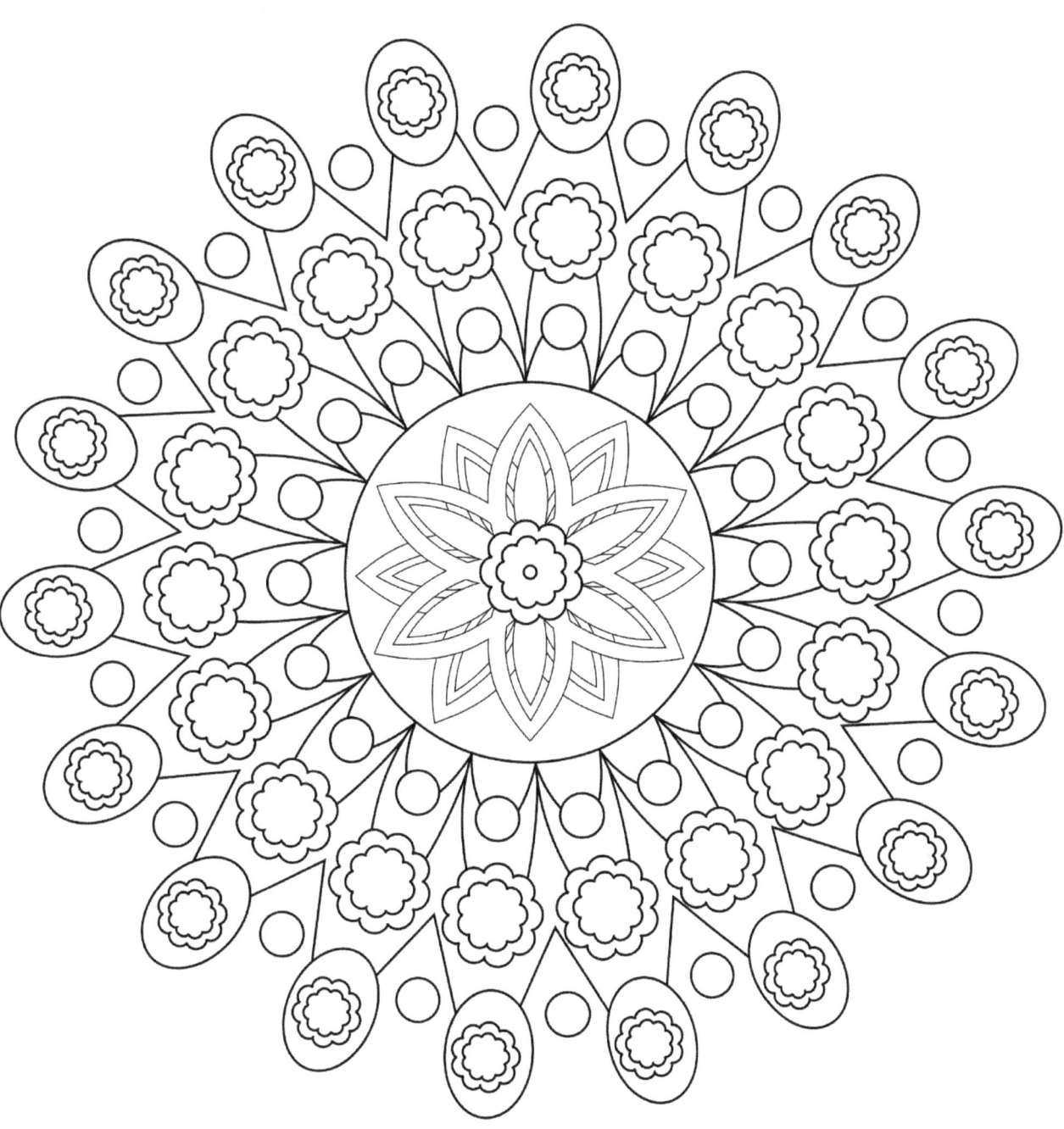

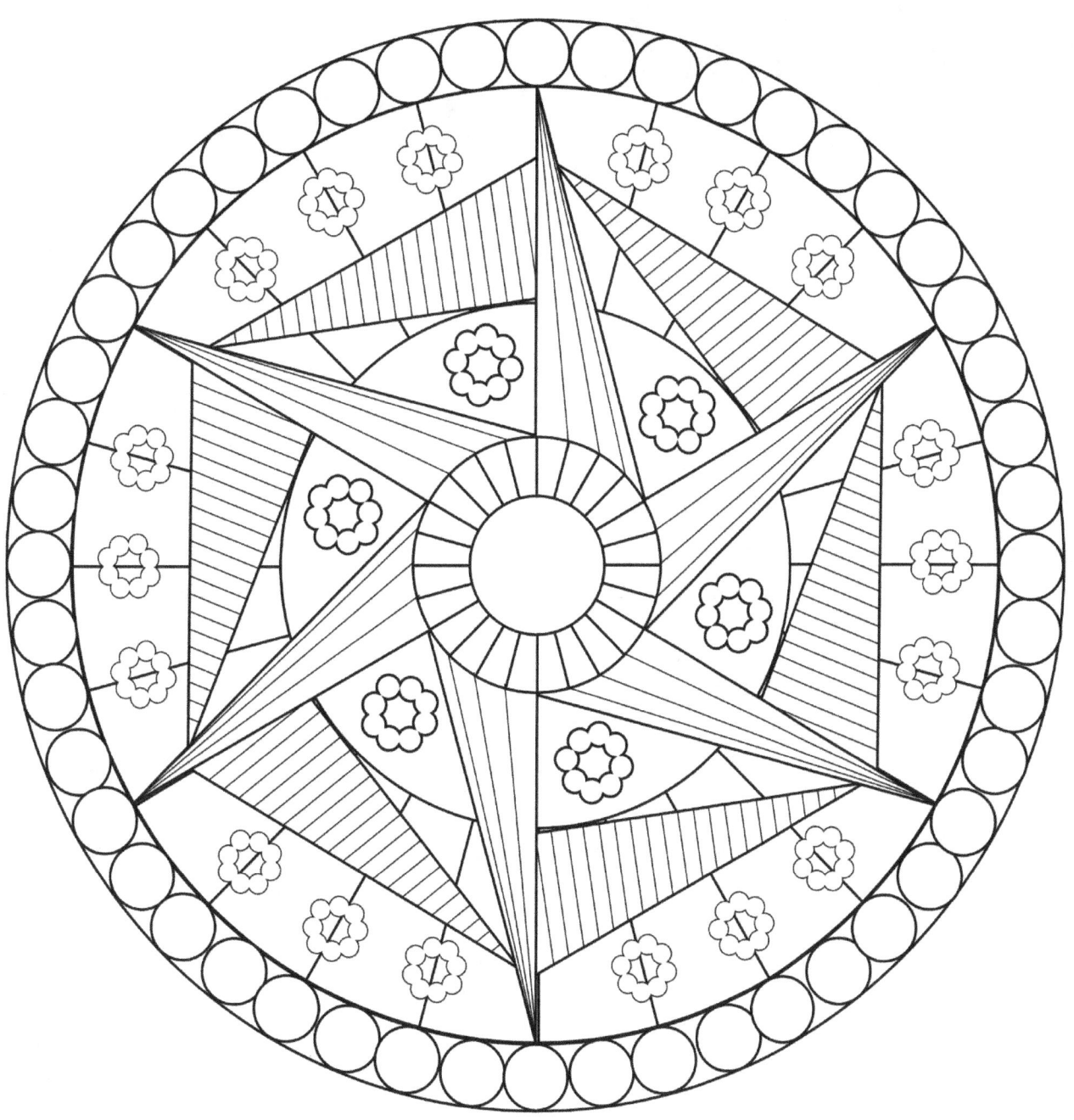

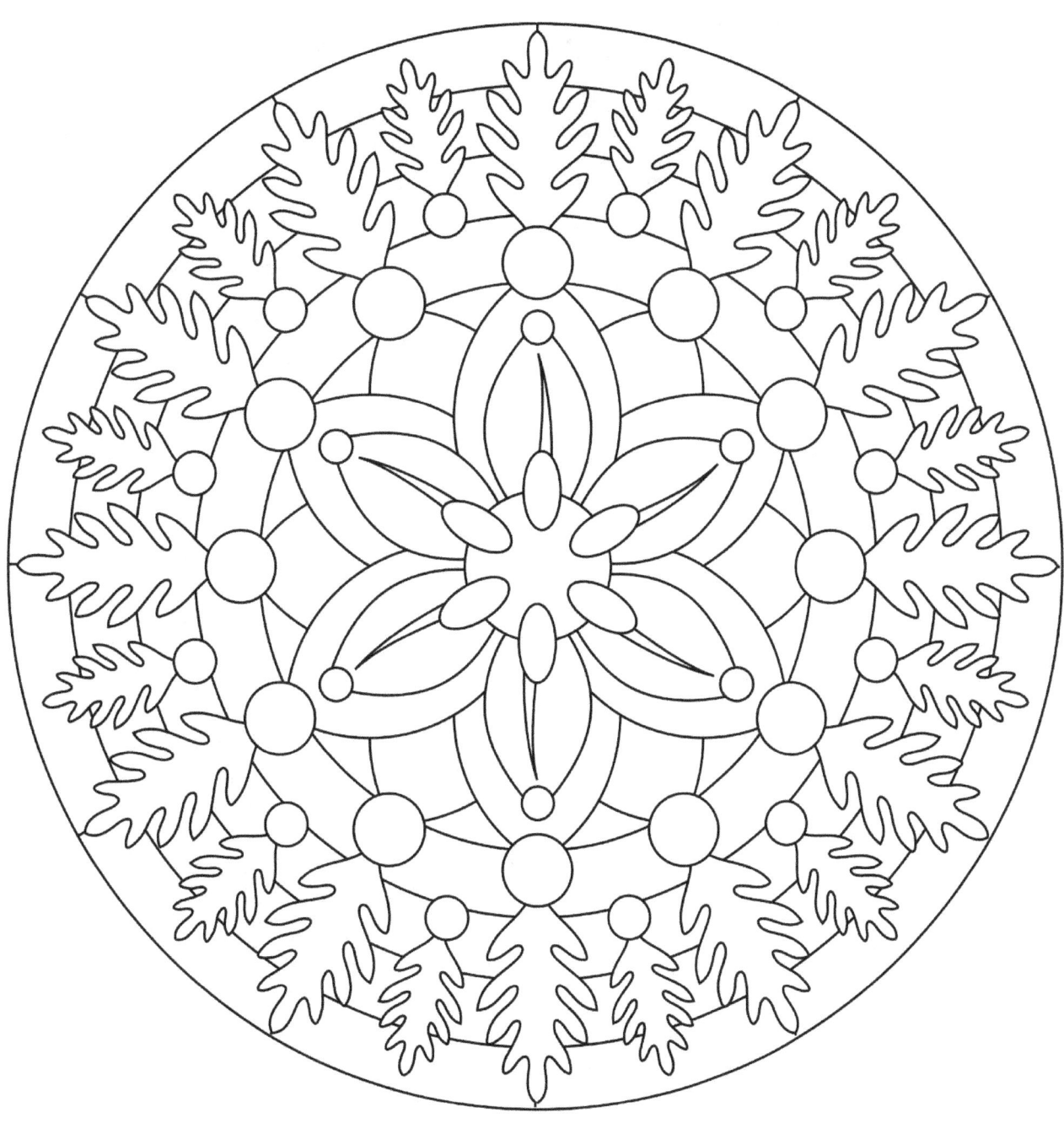

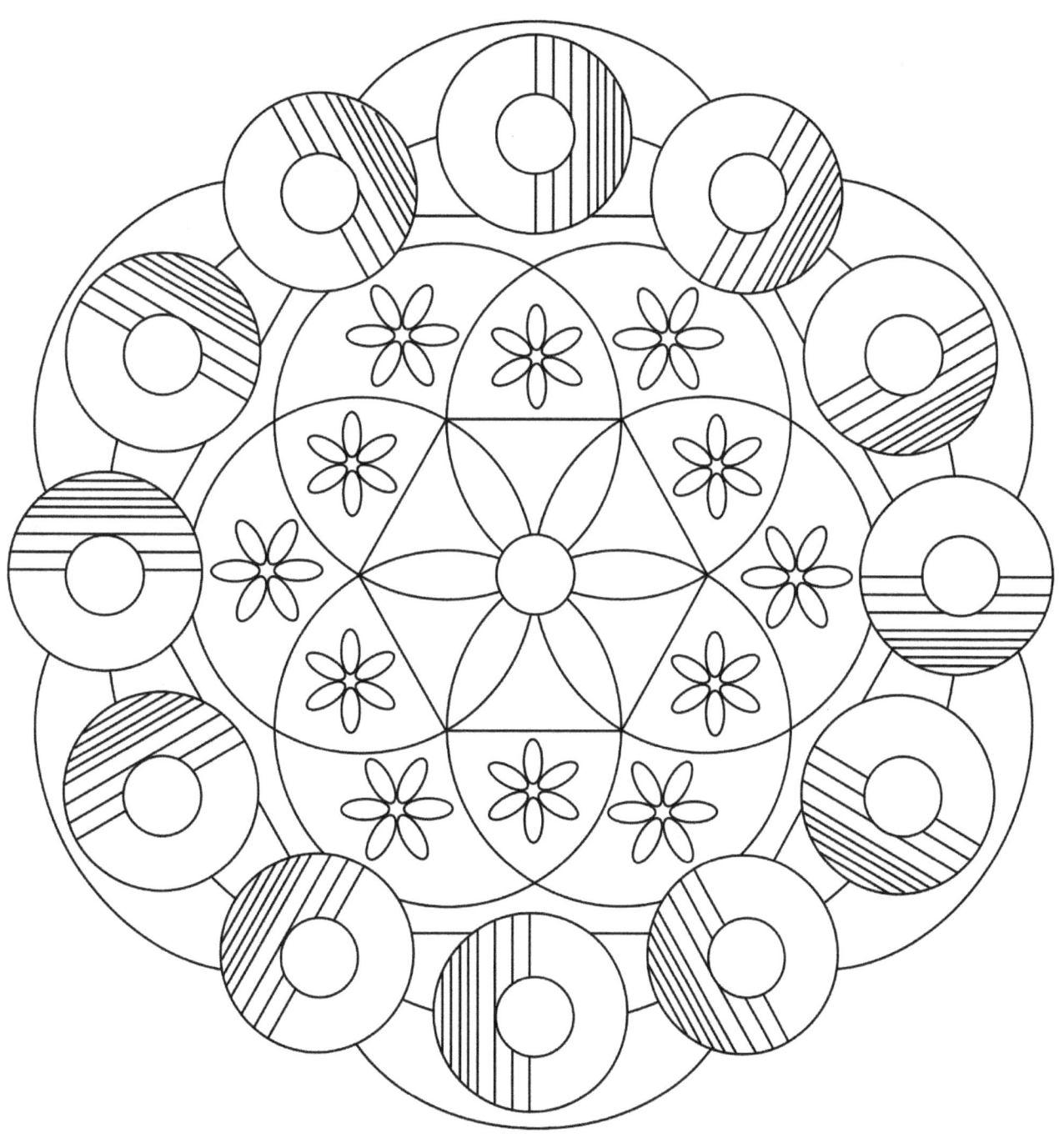

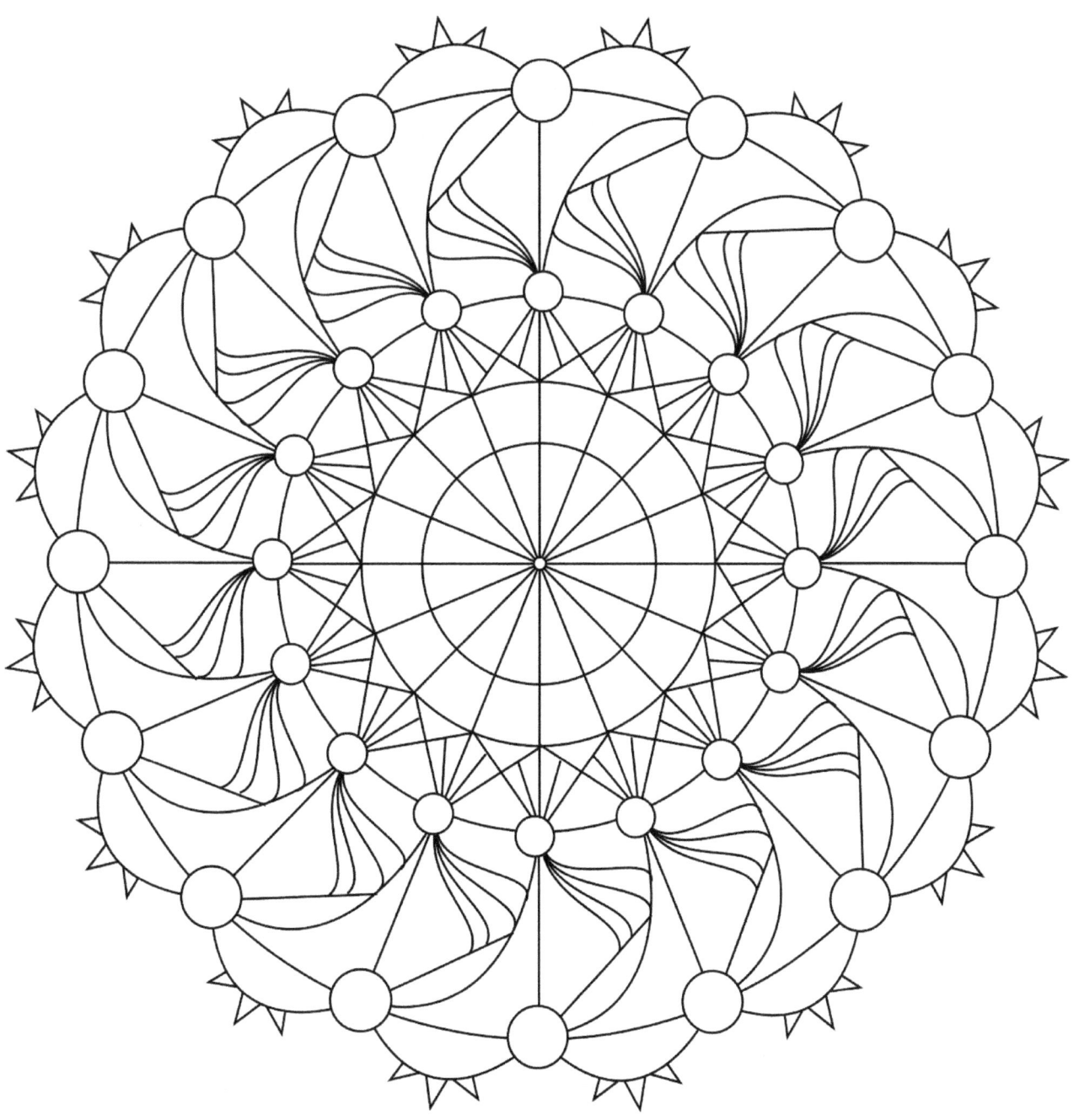

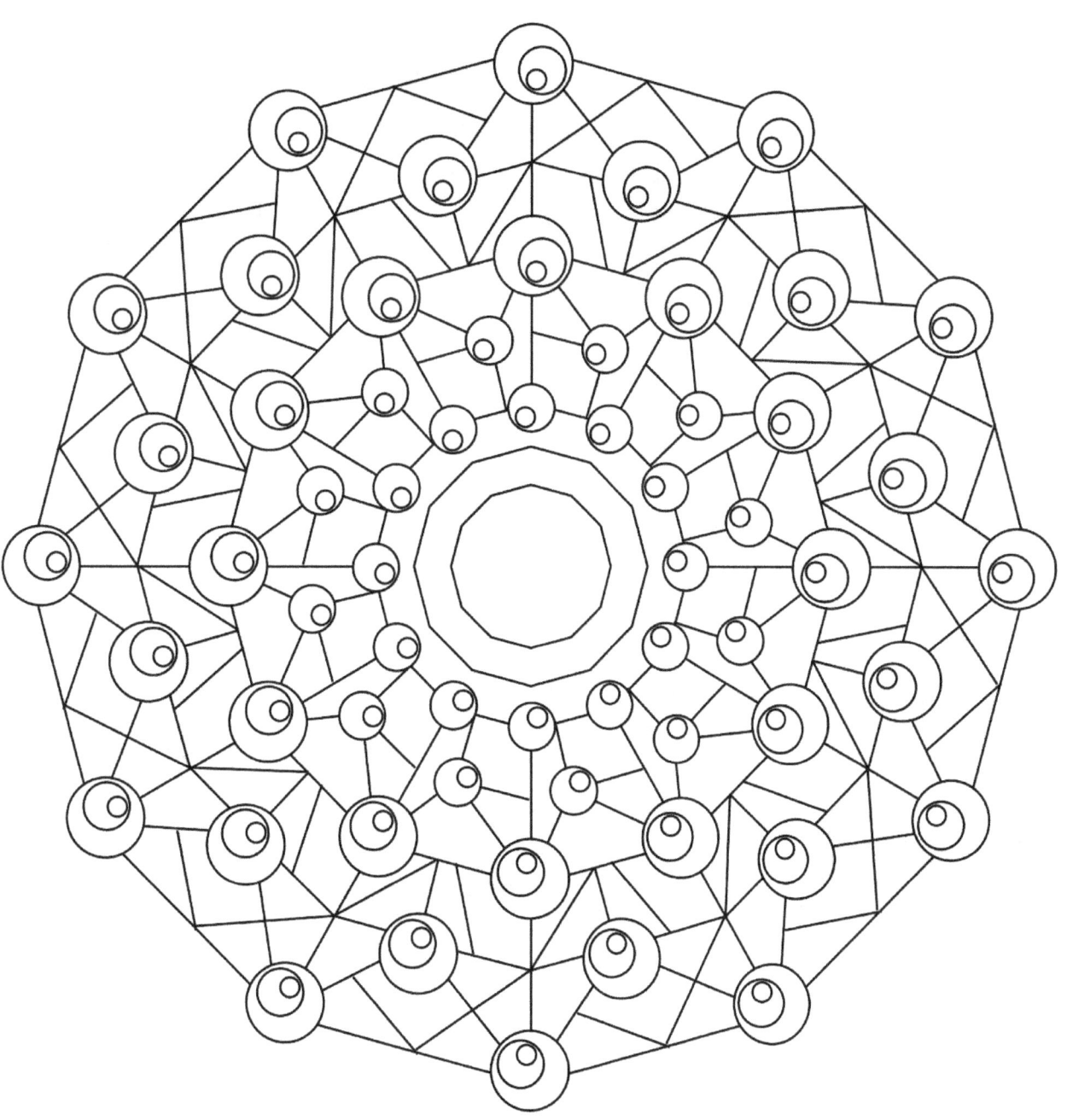

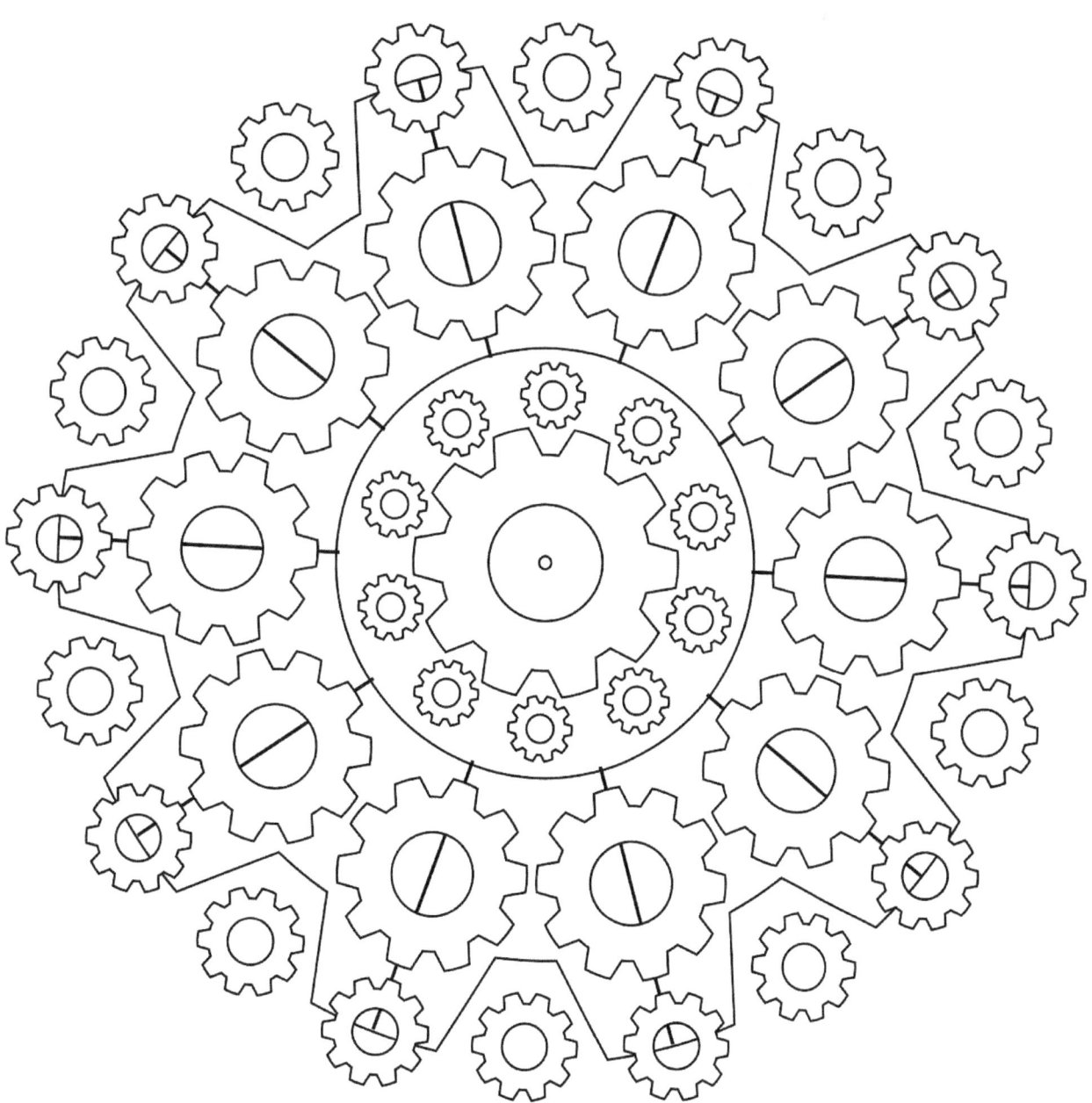

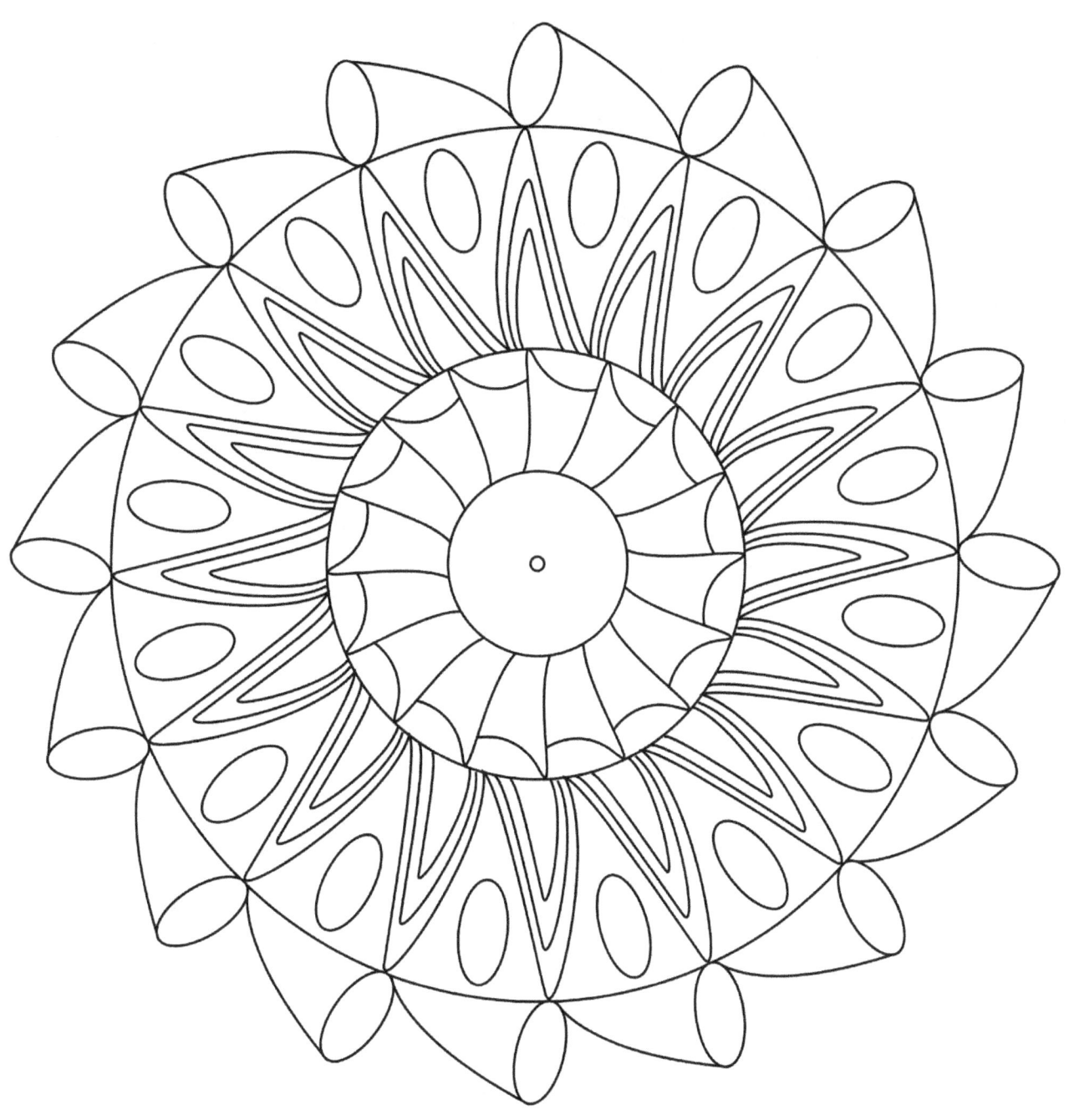

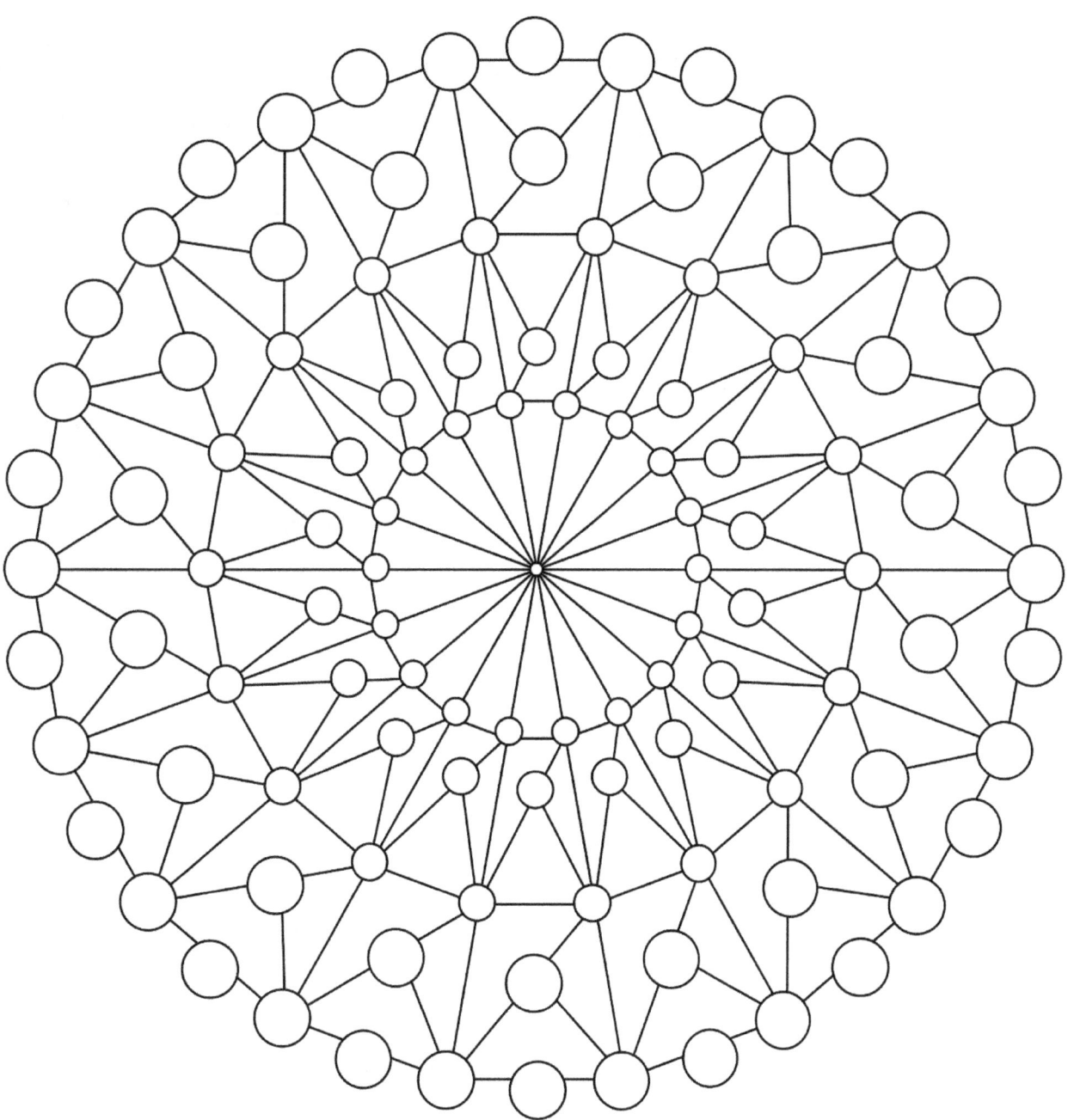

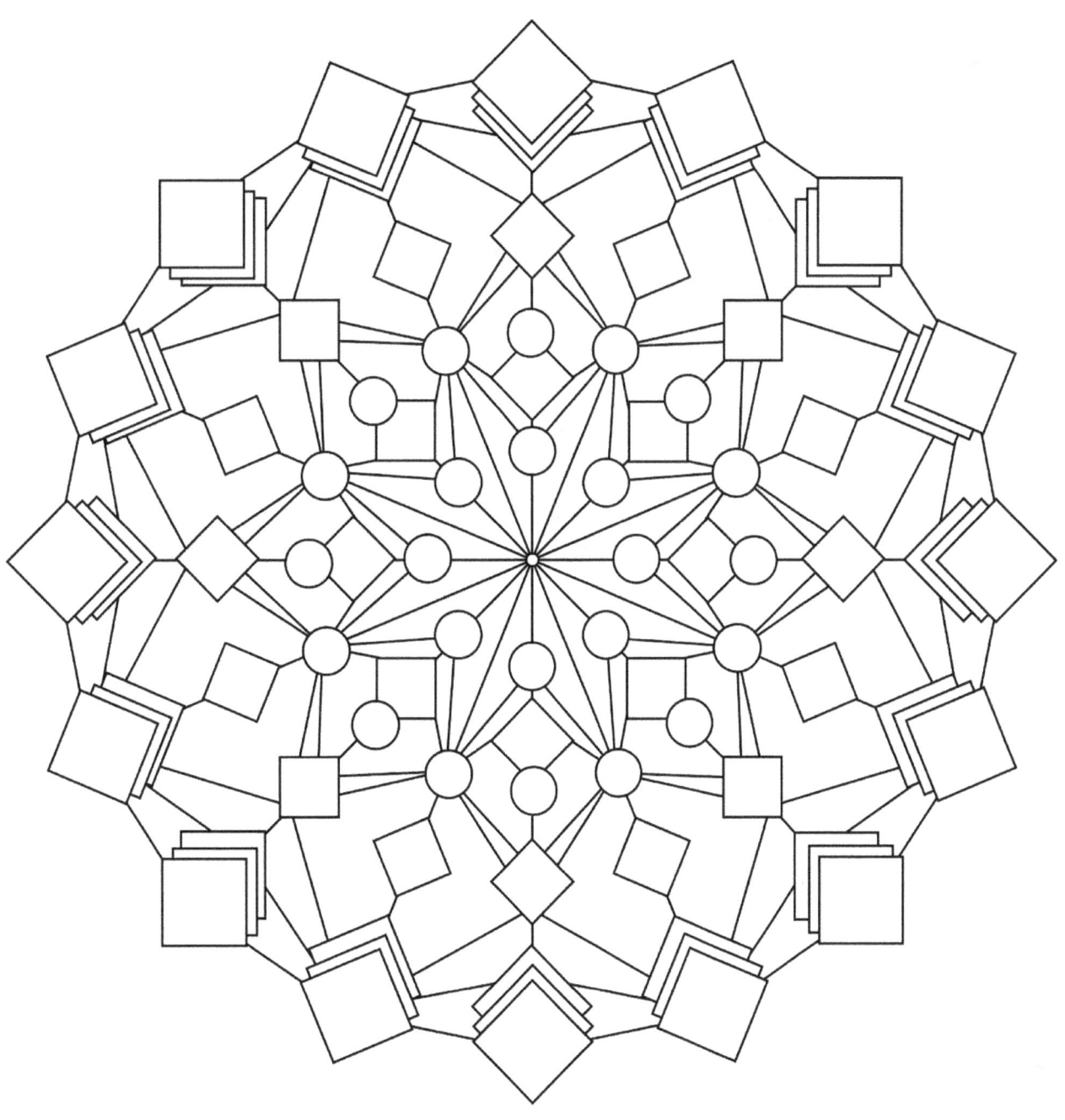

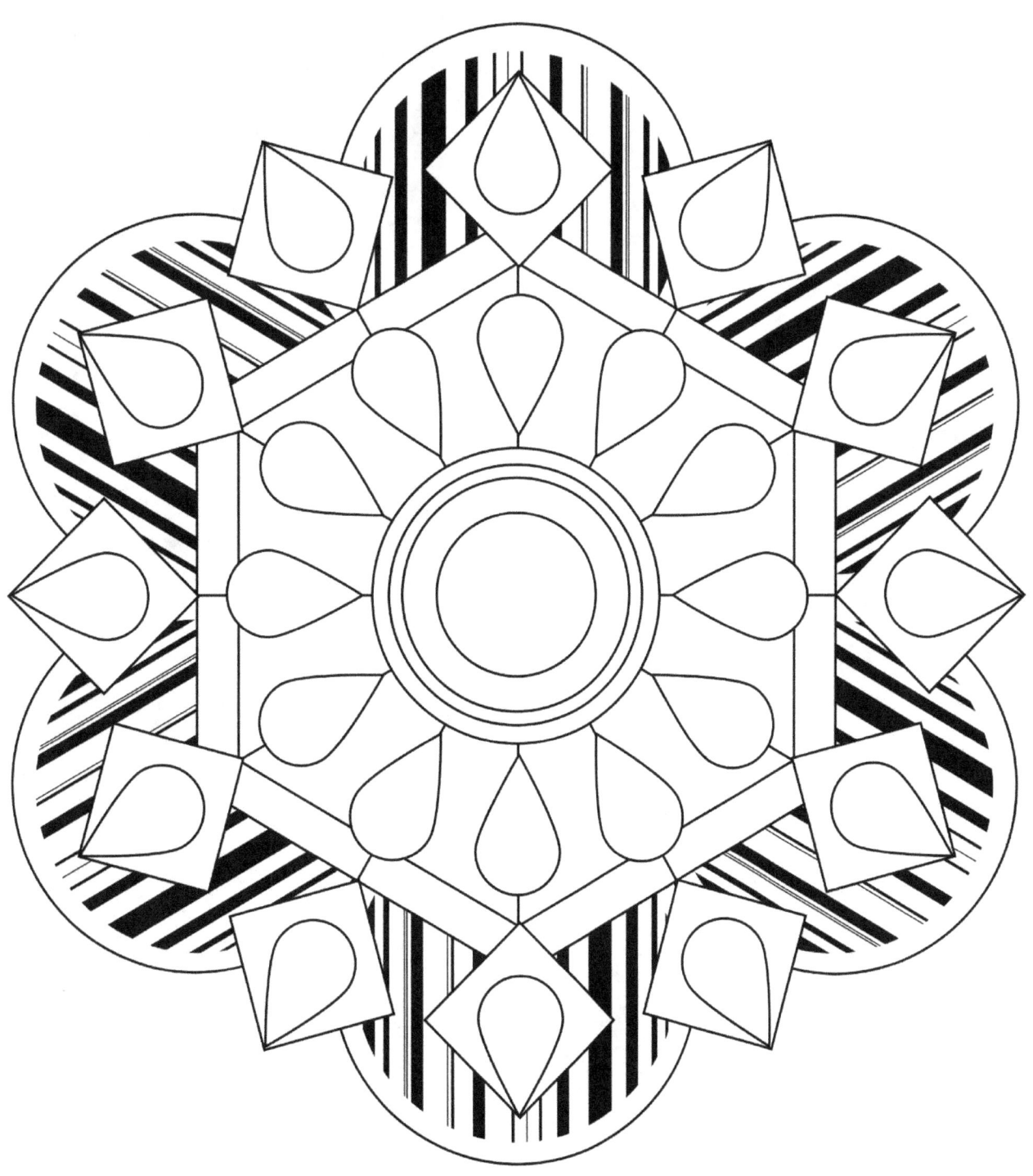

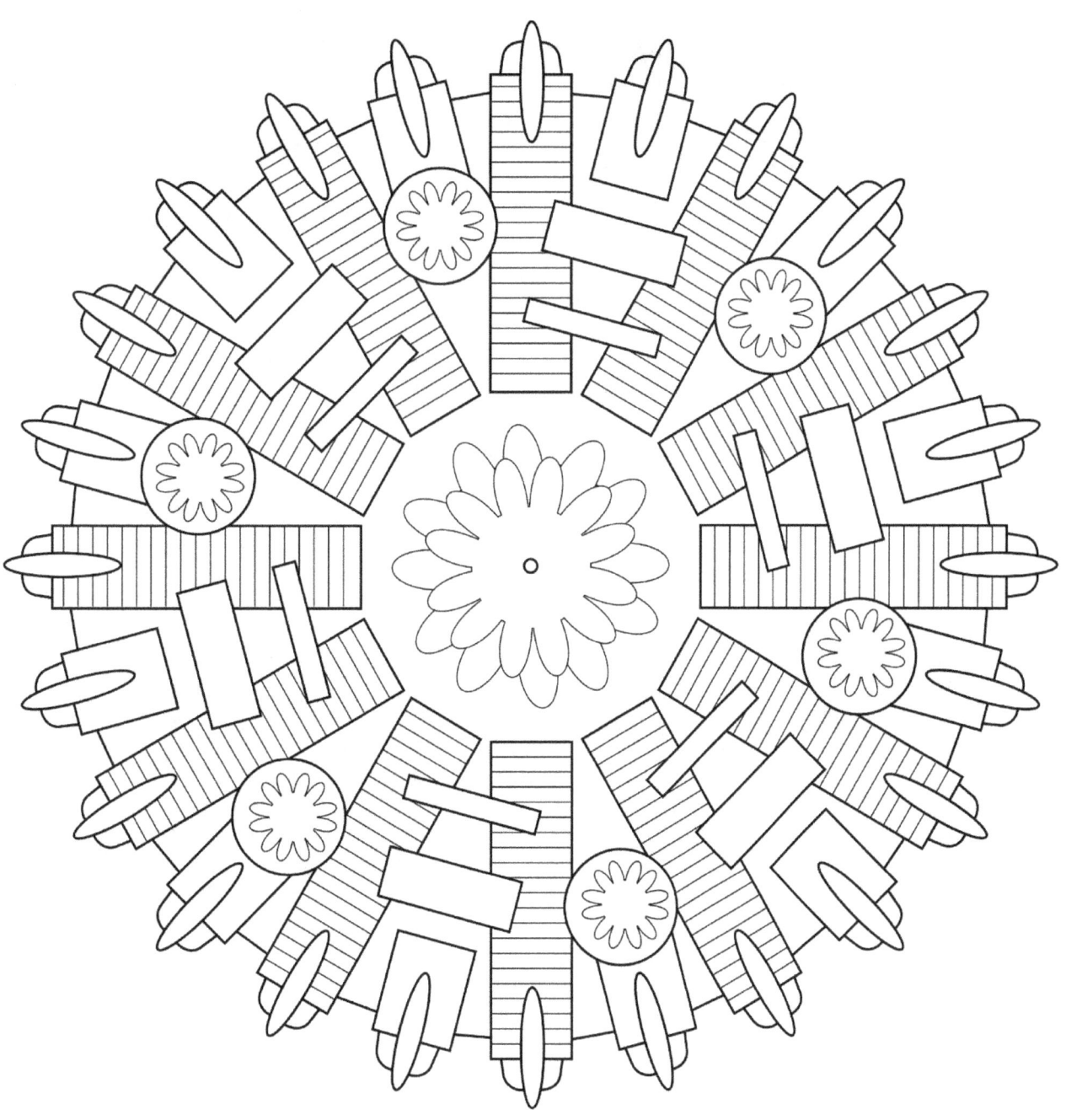

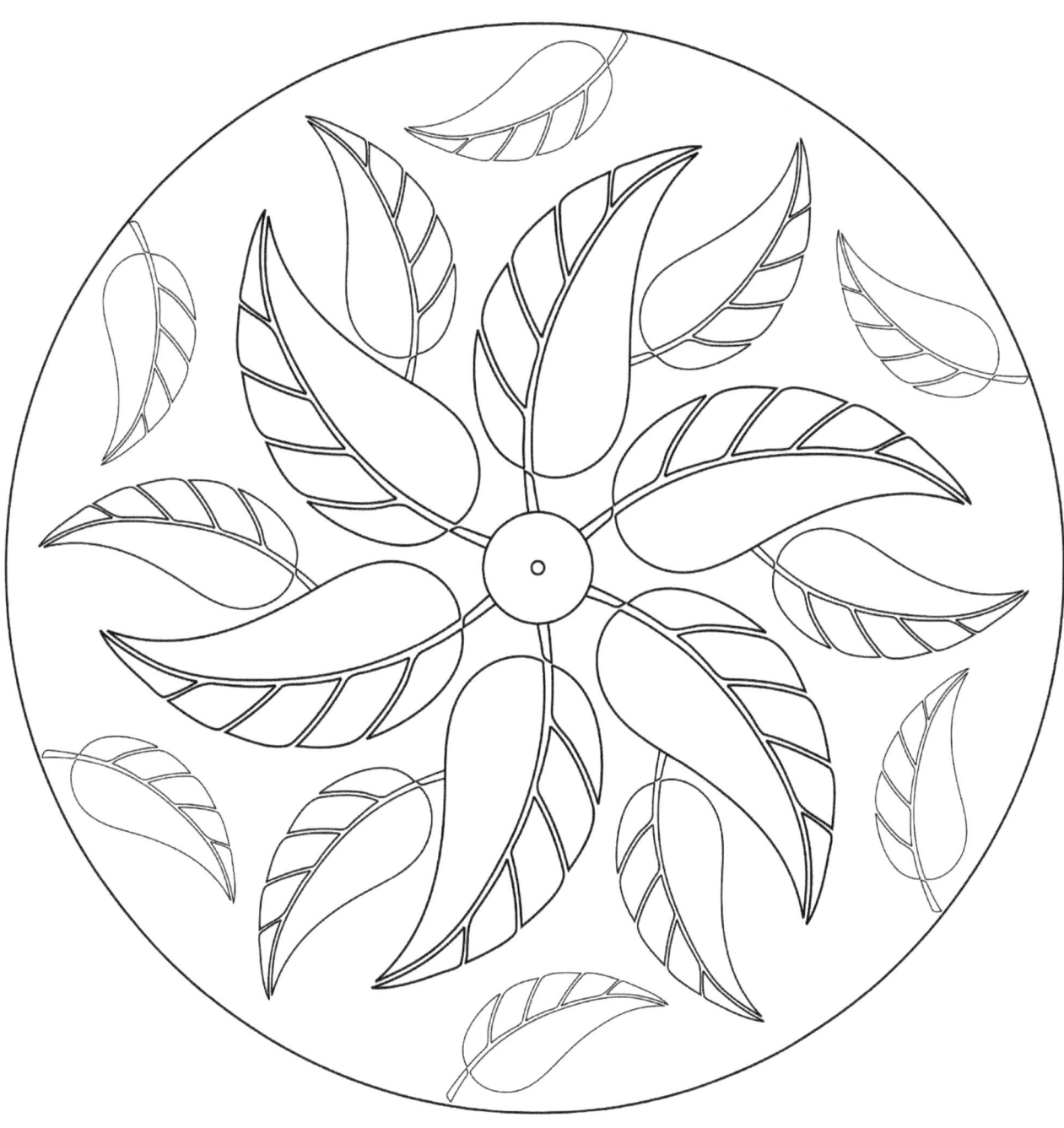

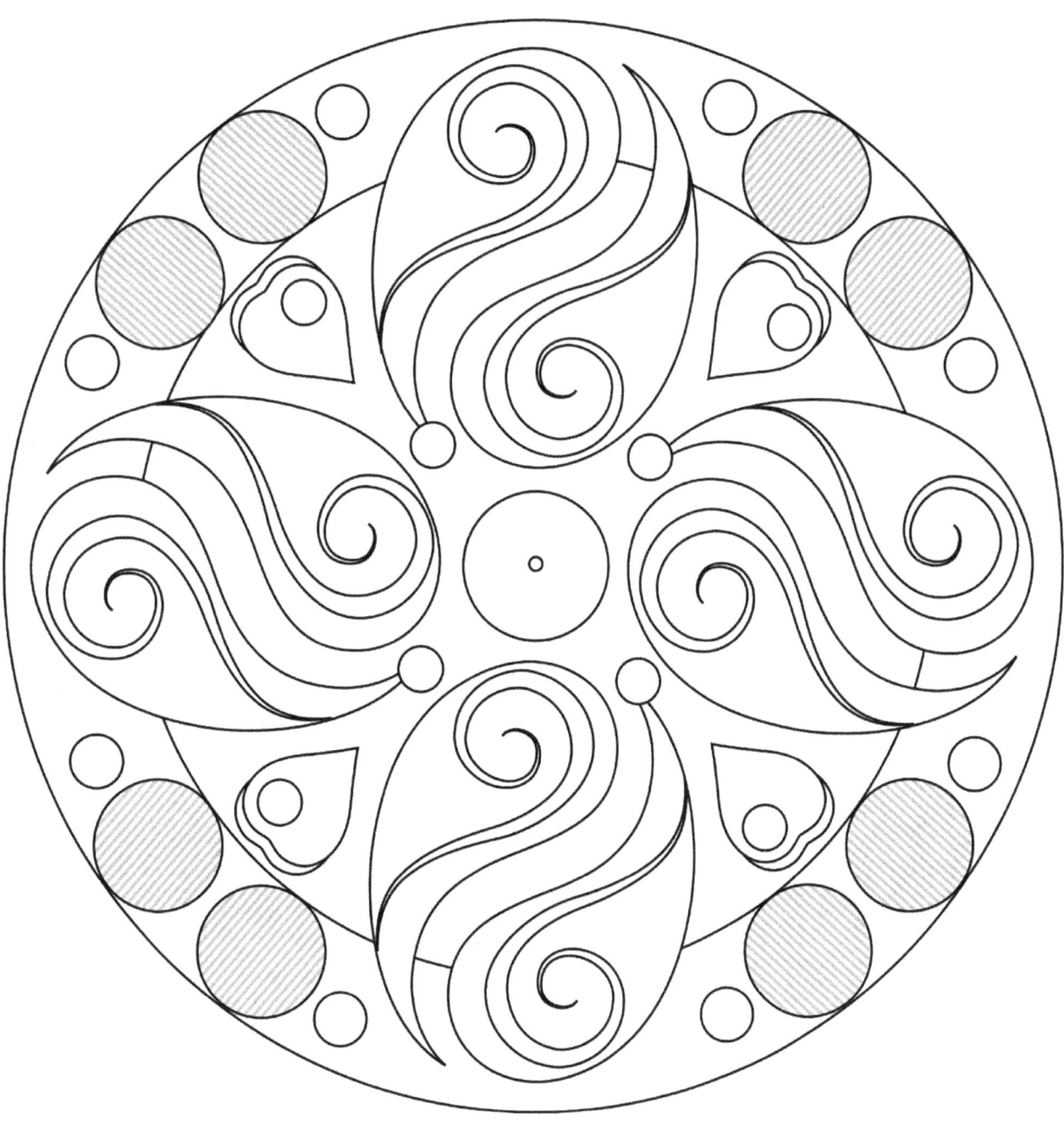

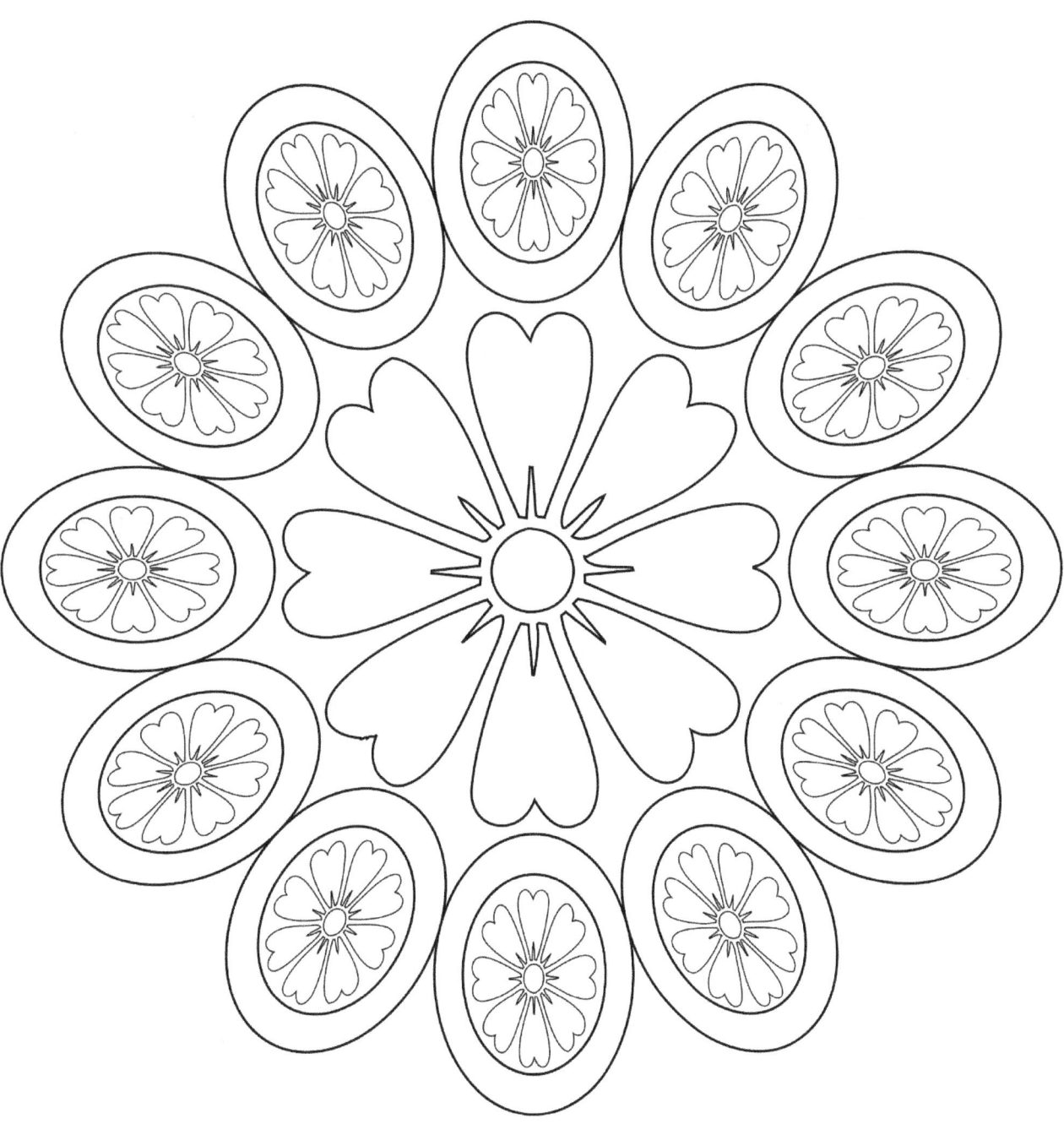

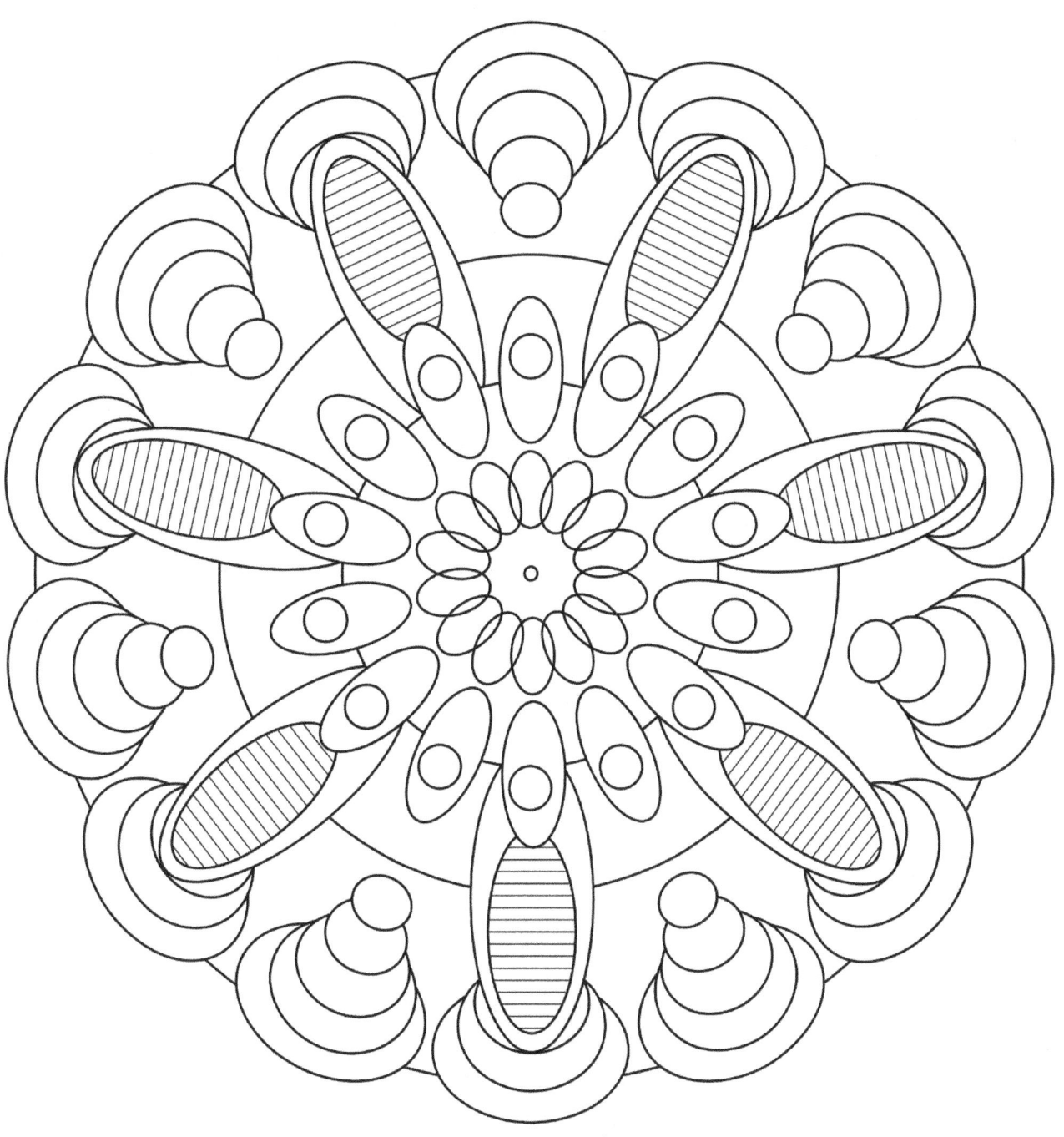

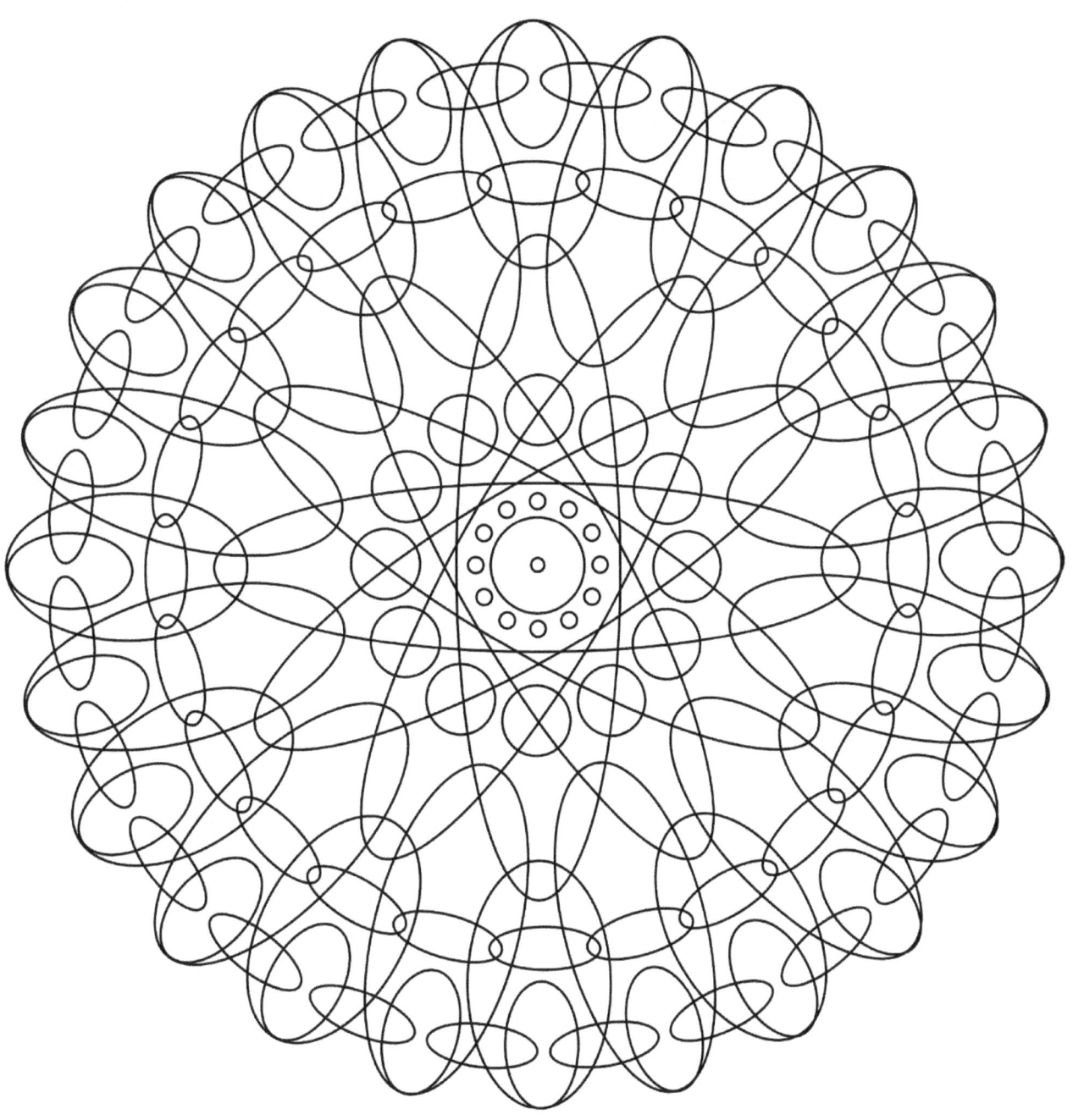

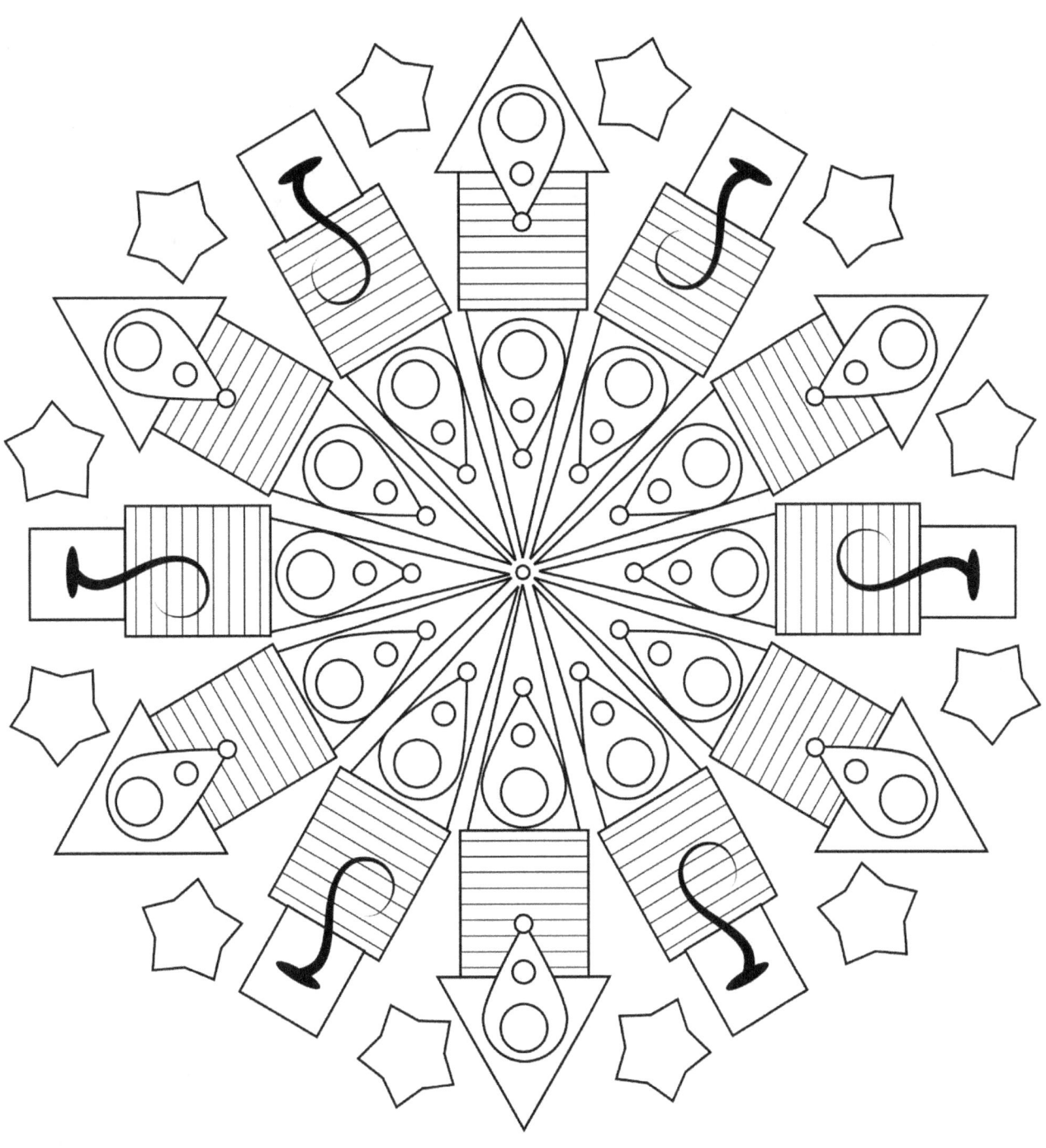